SHORT, SHARP AND OFF THE POINT

SHORT, SHARP
AND OFF THE POINT

The Art of Good (and bad) Preaching

Robert Paterson

A ministry of World Vision

MARC
EUROPE

Paterson, Robert
  Short, sharp and off the point.
  1. Preaching
  I. Title
  251   BV4211.2

  ISBN 0–947697–50–0

MARC Europe is an integral part of World Vision, an international Christian humanitarian organisation. MARC's object is to assist Christian leaders with factual information surveys, management skills, strategic planning and other tools for evangelism. MARC Europe also publishes and distributes related books on matters of mission, church growth, management, spiritual maturity and other topics.

Copyright © 1987 by Robert M E Paterson.
      First published 1987.
      ISBN 0–947697–50–0
Printed in Britain for MARC, a division of Kingsway Publications, Lottbridge Drove, Eastbourne, East Sussex BN23 6NT by Anchor Brendon Ltd, Tiptree, Colchester, Essex CO5 0HD. Typeset in Sabon Roman by Watermark, Hampermill Cottage, Watford WD1 4PL. Covers printed by Creative Print and Design, Unit 2/3 Saxon Way, Trading Estate, Harmondsworth, Mx UB7 0LW.

DEDICATION

For Pauline, Simeon, Naomi and Rebecca
and for the many people who have had a hand
in the thankless task of helping me to preach
Ad majorem Dei gloriam!

CONTENTS

FROM REVELATION CHAPTERS 2 AND 3

Who hears? Do you
or I hear anything
but silence
or shouting
or noise?
Is it our own voices
we hear?
Or do we hear
him speak?

Who speaks? What does
he say today:
this voice,
this fire,
this wind,
this stirring of the air
after the dove?
He speaks of sorrow
and of joy.

Who listens? His word
rebukes and urges,
but lovingly.
You are
lukewarm,
have lost your love and trust,
past glories!
Listen! He speaks.
He tells of victory.

FOREWORD

'The Devil has just told me that!' retorted a preacher, on being congratulated in the church porch on the excellence of his sermon. But I think to the majority of us preachers, the Devil rarely whispers in congratulatory terms. At least not today.

Two hundred years ago, what was there, aesthetically, to compete with preaching? George Whitefield would ride into town, and like magic the fields would become deserted, with every able-bodied person off to hear the sermon. And indeed, for the average Pastor, what was there to do *but* preach? In 1743, when William Grimshaw became Vicar of Haworth, he would develop two weekly rounds of preaching. One was his 'Lazy Week', in which he preached from 12–14 times; his other week giving him some 20 or 30 occasions for preaching.

Life is faster and busier today—and more committee-ridden! Today's preacher is sucked into a vortex of administration, phone calls, interviews and correspondence. It is not too surprising that over the past few decades preaching has tended to take a back seat. Can this trend be reversed?

Here is a book written by a man with a passion for preaching—but who understands the world of TV, video, and the computer disk. Allow your self to fall in love with Robert Paterson's enthusiasm, his cascade of stories and his friendly counsel—and see if the spark of the preacher's call doesn't become fanned into incandescence. We who are preachers must believe that the tide is coming in again....

Richard Bewes
All Souls Church
Langham Place
London

Chapter 1

A NON-PROPHET-MAKING ORGANISATION

Have you ever been to one of those awful church meetings (which even the best churches have, or so I'm told) when you wonder whether everyone is deaf—everyone except you of course? Your church council is discussing something as vital and all-embracing as 'The Mission of the Church in our Area', and the chairman has his work cut out to keep the discussion on the subject. Mrs Honeysuckle wants to discuss the flower rota and why the Granny Club needs yet another key to the hall. George Verity is worried about whether the new pulpit-fall is scriptural and whether we're on a slippery slope of some sort. Elizabeth Sanctity tells everyone about a book she's been reading that answered all her problems, and all we need to do is have more prayer meetings. Alfred Downspout is most concerned about a damp patch in church that he's seen spreading throughout the winter. Young Jimmy Keen keeps saying that mission means evangelism, and we ought to have a campaign. Seven councillors haven't said a word because they're afraid of offending old Mr Badger, a church officer, who jumps in quickly with a word of caution and chips in with the odd remark about past glories. Mr Grind, the lay preacher, thinks it would be better if we were to return to three services on Christmas morning for the sake of people who come occasionally. Dr Lee Ann tells the council once more that they are all too middle-class and not concerned about 'the real issues'. (Besides, she hasn't time to waste—she's flying to the Greek islands tomorrow for two weeks' holiday.) The other six are obviously confused. The chairman, who happens to be the minister, looks depressed.

If you don't recognise that meeting, you are very lucky! If you've never experienced one like it, you have that treat in store, with all the tragic disillusionment it brings. At one level, it's perfectly natural that a well-balanced committee should have delightful variations in personality and approach—that's all to the good. The real problem is that the committee doesn't know where to begin! It lacks a basic Christian map—a theological map, if you'll pardon the expression; it's confused about the scope of mission and is wandering about aimlessly in its attempts to discover where it should go next. Some gentle education in the way a council works may help our poor minister, but the fundamental solution to the problem lies in his hands. That church needs consistent teaching and stimulus for service: it needs a prophet! And what is a prophet? He or she is one who carefully and fearlessly proclaims God's intentions for today and passes on the divine command: *'Listen to the word of the Lord!'*

The prophets of the Old Testament spoke that word of command from God, calling on the people to listen and to act. Isaiah, a man accustomed to leadership, had a message from the holy God to deliver about the path of redemptive suffering. Jeremiah, the reluctant hero who didn't want to be a prophet, doubted and questioned his calling when faced with persecution, a man of granite with the heart of a child, delivering God's message of judgement and hope to his people. Ezekiel, a prophet with a message of judgement and hope, preached not only of national but also personal renewal for the people of God. Amos, the layman and missionary with the fire of God in his belly, found himself preaching fearlessly to wanton greed and careless morality. Hosea, the gentle husband of a whore, became the messenger of God's forgiving and renewing love. These men were rarely successful, except perhaps with a few, but they were faithful to their calling. Ezekiel's call is typical:

> Mortal man, I am sending you to the people of Israel.
> They have rebelled and turned against me and are still
> rebels, just as their ancestors were. They are stubborn
> and do not respect me, so I am sending you to tell them
> what I, the Sovereign Lord, am saying to them.
> Whether those rebels listen to you or not, they will
> know that a prophet has been among them. But you,
> mortal man, must not be afraid of them or of anything
> they say. They will defy and despise you; it will be like
> living among scorpions... You will tell them whatever
> I tell you to say, whether they listen or not... none of
> the people of Israel will be willing to listen; they will
> not even listen to me. All of them are stubborn and
> defiant. Now I will make you as stubborn and as tough
> as they are.   (Ezekiel 2:3–7; 3:7–8)

And this is but a sample.

Our Lord Jesus himself was called a prophet by those who witnessed his ministry: 'A great prophet has appeared among us!', the people said, full of fear and praise at the raising of a dead boy (Luke 7:16). 'God has come to save his people!' Even the most casual reading of the four Gospels shows us the Son of God deeply concerned to communicate truth—truth about God, truth about humanity, and the need to act on that truth. Can you imagine the indignation of the religious leaders, the professionals, hearing the prophetic word of Jesus?

> You snakes and sons of snakes! How do you expect to
> escape from being condemned to hell? And so I tell you
> that I will send you prophets and wise men and
> teachers; you will kill some of them, crucify others,
> and whip others in the synagogues and chase them
> from town to town.   (Matthew 23:33–34)

No doubt it was easier for Jesus to be a prophet than anyone else: he is the Son of God, his very existence is a prophetic word, a word from the Lord; he is the eternal Word of God, and his presence uniquely draws back the curtain and shows us God. Other prophets have to take more care!

It is difficult to say how the Church of New Testament times viewed the prophetic ministry: the apostle Paul places the gift of prophecy very high on his lists of Spirit-filled ministries and longs for all God's people to have this ministry (I Corinthians 14:1). At a more formal level, 'prophets' seem to belong to an established order of ministry in the youthful Christian Church second only to apostles. Sometimes they are heard predicting the future, but this seems to be a rare form of their calling, since their work was to preach the word of the Lord to their own day. They encouraged, strengthened and comforted the people of God; they preached the gospel of sin and judgement, grace and mercy. (See Acts 11:28; 15:32; I Corinthians 12:28–29; 14:24–25.) In many ways, these prophets were forerunners of ordained Christian ministry.

PROPHETS TODAY

The Spirit-inspired prophetic ministry—'Listen to the word of the Lord!'—must be supported and fed by a systematic teaching of Christian truth, and that means, at the very least, helping the people of God to become familiar with the Scriptures of the Old and New Testaments. Whilst the word of the Lord can be and sometimes is heard in a theological vacuum, the Church has always sought to test prophecy by referring to the Bible and to the known life of the Holy Spirit in the Church. As Christians, we believe in the God who reveals himself to us, so we must take seriously the person who tells us that he's had a special message from God. However, I recall an incident when an otherwise orthodox Christian supposed he had received a 'special message from the Lord' which, in short, left Christ not only bereft of his divinity but also a sinner! His prophecy had to be called to order by the Bible.

Again, in a popular London church a stranger presented himself in the vestry before worship to tell the vicar that the Lord had given him a word to speak on that day, and that therefore he intended to preach. 'How strange!', the vicar replied. 'I was under the impression that he had given *me* a word to speak today.' To some, that may seem cynical and a suppression of the Spirit, but the visitor's prophecy had to be called to order by the known ways of the Holy Spirit within the Church: the vicar's response served to underline that prophecy and regular, systematic teaching are normally found hand-in-hand. Certainly, in churches all over our nation, the crying need is not for peripatetic prophets but for faithful preachers who will teach and proclaim the word of the Lord for today.

But what has all this to do with Mrs Honeysuckle and Mr Downspout and their friends, let alone the poor parson? Their real problem is that they've been fed with bits and pieces of God-talk (theology). Because it doesn't all fit together for them, they can't remember much of what they've heard. And because they've had some teaching in the past, they think they have heard all anyone needs to hear, so they don't listen when God speaks to them in the present!

Their need for a prophet can substantially be met by a good ministry of preaching. They believe in the education of their children, providing them with a basic foundaton of literacy, numeracy and so on, in the hope that the habit of learning may not be lost entirely in adulthood. But their own Christian education has been limited to a smattering at school (of uncertain quality—it depends on the school), perhaps some kind of adult church membership course (possibly, nay probably, given too young and too briefly), very small doses of daily Bible reading (for those who are really devout) and little formal teaching of the faith during worship. And because the preacher assumes his work is undervalued, he neglects it and the downward spiral continues. Dr Donald Coggan has warned us of the danger of rearing a generation of Christians... foreigners to the many great truths of the Christian faith. They have never had the opportunity of listening, Sunday by Sunday, to a steady, intelligent, interesting exposition of the things most surely believed among us... They dare not speak, lest they make fools of themselves... They are spiritual Peter Pans.[1]

And we may remember the necessary ingredient in Peter Pan's recipe for flying: 'Think a happy thought! Any happy little thought will do.'

If our Church Council has a problem, it may be because Parson Snuffle and his colleagues have neglected their preaching ministry, because they've been struggling to define their own ministry for many years, not helped by the rapid pace of change today, nor by their people's reluctance to see what's been happening. Right across denominational lines, the Church has tended to define its ministry mainly in terms of what pastors may do that others may not, and these definitions usually owe more to the past than to the present. In short, the Church selects its ministers carefully, accepting their call from God, trains them rigorously in certain specialist ministries and then ordains them. At that point, their pastoral specialism is transformed into that of an ordained watering-can, sprinkling God's pastoral favour on the largest number of people who can be sprinkled upon in their homes; their leadership specialism is called to account by the likes of Mr Badger and Mr Verity who know much less about Church leadership than they realise; and their preaching specialism (the most particular specialism of all) is squeezed out by the pressures of time or so under-rated by the people that the clergy themselves come to accept its low value.

The same problem arises with lay preachers or readers who are often trained in only a few areas of theology, and given little precept or practice of preaching beyond an imitation of their local pastor—who may not be very good at it! They are often men and women who lead busy lives—indeed they usually are—who can afford too little time for initial training and rarely have much desire for in-service training or even retraining. 'Re-training?', a friend once asked me when I had suggested my need. '*Restraining*, more like!'

When I was rector in a delightful part of the Welsh countryside, my parishes consisted of two villages and their surrounding countryside, with a total population of around 2,000 and, perhaps 8 miles or so from end to end. In addition, I had the privilege of helping to initiate some overseas mission work in that diocese. One generation earlier, each village had its own rector and a population of around 300. In the early 1950s, one rector to 300 parishioners; in the late 1970s, two-thirds of a rector to 2,000 people in two villages. Given the real contact a country parson has with all the people of his parish, it's no wonder he feels pushed when a well-meaning lady (who remembers the old days) asks him why he doesn't drop in on all the children's birthday parties! And if the rural parson has problems, his urban counterpart has at least as many, often struggling to serve a big church in a deprived inner-city area (or in self-contented suburbia), equipped with totally inadequate buildings, a burden of administration, and insufficient lay leadership. In both city and country, the minister easily becomes the safety net for the local church, supposedly doing what the rest of the Church can't or won't do!

THE SQUEEZE

Now this is not a book about how busy the ministers and lay workers of the Church are, so why is the fact important? The answer is quite close at hand: if you are busy, if you have too much to do, what gives? In most cases, it's the preparation. There's a true saying in the army that 'reconnaissance is worth a thousand men'. If you're a busy home-maker, it may be the new ideas in the kitchen that you shelve; if you're in industrial management, it may be the report you know you ought to commission but you dread the thought of all that extra work; if you're a busy gardener, it's planning out the new rockery that's going to take time when you should be planting the spuds; and if you're a busy preacher, the pressure is on the preaching—at least, it's on the time for study and preparation. That's also the *easy* way. The home-maker will get away with the same old menus week after week; the manager will keep the firm ticking over with no great crisis, at least until he or she retires; the garden will look fine without the rockery, and home-grown potatoes will save money; the congregation won't notice the slack preparation because preaching rates pretty low for them and their priority for the preacher would be the social work he does.

> I think preachers are getting lost in a multitude of smaller duties. The preacher has a peculiar place in the economy of God. He is in danger of becoming so involved with secondary affairs that he loses his prophetic gift. The devil doesn't care how great a success a preacher is in any other field, if he can just kill the prophet in him.[2]

The vicar's little daughter asked, 'Why does Daddy say a prayer before his sermons?'

'So that God will help him when he's preaching,' came Mummy's stock answer.

'So why doesn't he?'

Probably because he needs more time to prepare, or he needs help with his technique, or his first love is burning low. Preachers under pressure usually let their high standards of preaching go at an early stage, not because they want to, but because they have to. They soon discover that the short, pithy one-idea sermon is the one which comes to them most easily on a Saturday night.

The next stage is to realise that the short sermon has a lot of force when it's sharp and practical and topical. Few realise that the short sermon can contain a lot more if it is well-constructed, but this kind of writing and the power to listen so attentively are both dying arts. So what's the result? One-off talks on some issue of the day tacked onto a biblical text (a pre-text), or second-rate versions of the leading article in the current church weekly newspaper—as the compliment of a Northamptonshire churchgoer a few years ago revealed: 'Nice sermon. Short, sharp and off the point!'[3] So often these sermons simply moralise about what to do in life's difficulties without helping the people to understand why they should do it: they become 'helpful hints for harmful habits'![4] The faithful who gather week by week to praise, to pray, to celebrate, to unite in Christ, need better and more consistent feeding in God's truth and a clearer prophetic challenge to serve him in the world.

THEOLOGY, ANYONE?

Why can't Parson Snuffle get his people along to a home group, or to regard worship as top priority, or to see mission in its broadest terms, or to want to share the Gospel? They'll tell him if he asks the right questions—they're not interested in the thing they call 'theology'! But, without an attack of dry rot or deathwatch beetle, just watch what happens if he suggests moving some pews from the back of the church building: the theologians appear out of the woodwork as if by magic, all keen to lecture him in a whole library's worth of systematic folk-theology!

And why is the church council so divided between people obsessed with gutters and downspouts and people obsessed with pie in the sky? Because their grasp of the breadth of Christian truth is so limited. They suffer from an ecclesiastical bicycle shed mentality, like the board of directors of a multinational company which passes a £500,000 advertising campaign on the nod because they've been advised to do it and don't really understand it; but ask them to spend a few hundred pounds on a bicycle shed and, far worse, ask them where it should be put, and you could be in for a six-hour debate! They don't understand the big issues, and the only ones they can talk about are the trivial ones. What's worse is that they don't seem to realise that they have a problem.

In many if not most of our churches, people lack a basic map of the faith. All that many of them are getting is disconnected bits and pieces, sometimes good, sometimes pretty useless. They are confused and disorientated, and they are not listening for the voice of God. Robert Short[5] was right in his comments about *The Gospel According to Peanuts*: the Church may well be the world's largest non-prophet organisation—and it seems that it may be even worse now than it was when he wrote the comment in 1966.

NOTES

[1] Donald Coggan, *On Preaching* (SPCK: London, 1978), p 9.
[2] Vance Havner [source unknown] taken from Donald Coggan, *ibid*, pp 13–14
[3] Quoted from I D Bunting, *Preaching at Communion (i)* (Grove: Nottingham, 1981), p 22.
[4] *ibid*, p 6.
[5] Robert Short, *The Gospel According to Peanuts* (Collins Fontana: Great Britain, 1966), p 25.

Chapter 2

I'VE HEARD IT ALL BEFORE:
Mr Badger's Blindspot

Mr Badger's been going to church for most of his life. In the beginning it was Sunday school—his parents sent him and he rather liked it so he stayed on and went to church. Because he was brought up as a Baptist, he was baptised in his mid-teens along with his other friends in the youth Bible class and beforehand he was given a few basic lessons in the Christian faith by the minister. He was told, amongst other things, to pray every day, to read his Bible and to worship regularly. He couldn't really be described as one of the church's great successes, though he is in church virtually every Sunday and occasionally he'll go along to the Bible study, but I'm afraid he very rarely reads his Bible at home.

If he were to be asked for his opinions on his Christian faith, he'd say, 'Christianity is really a kind of religious common sense.' What that really means is not so much that he disagrees with Saint Paul but that he believes there are too many fanatics around and they're always quoting their Bibles—he wouldn't want to be like that! In fact, he's given up thinking Christianly and has given his own values and his own common sense the title of 'Christianity'.

I'm sorry to say that he's lost much of the freshness of his love for God and these days the only thing which could fan the embers of his faith into a few flickering flames is a chorus of *Onward, Christian Soldiers!* He has become very suspicious of Christians who can find the book of Ruth in the Bible without consulting the index, or of folk who can tell you the difference between John's Gospel and the letters of John; more seriously, these people have an outline of biblical history in their minds and they've obviously sorted out the basic biblical doctrines. Not so Mr Badger, and his failure to grasp the broad sweep of the Bible has turned a little sour. Yes, his love for God may well be quite genuine, and God's love for him is utterly certain, but he's lost when it comes to the Bible; he's lost when it comes to sorting out the basic Christian truths; and he's lost when it comes to sharing the faith of Christ with others.

He tries to listen to sermons, but they seem to wash over him. He often gets as much as halfway through, but the preachers keep saying things like, 'You remember the parable of the hidden treasure...', or 'I don't need to remind you of when God told Moses his special name...' Unfortunately Mr Badger doesn't remember the parable of the hidden treasure and, although he remembers the story of the burning bush that wasn't burned, he can't remember what was said. In fact, listening to sermons sometimes seems to him like playing with a one-arm bandit: when the preacher goes up into the pulpit it's like pulling the arm on the machine and all those difficult doctrines and names and books and characters go whizzing round like oranges and lemons and bells and plums, and he never seems to get the jackpot! The older he gets, the more he convinces himself that he's heard it all before. He must have been taught the basics of faith in Christ when he was baptised. He must have heard most of the Bible and all the important doctrines preached many times in the last 60 years. And, in a strange sort of way, sermons are still important to him at times, especially when he hears a stirring preacher and he leaves the church with something practical to think about. But for most of the time he's resigned to being theologically illiterate. What he needs is a consistent and persistent preacher.

There are many people in our churches today—I'd say *most* people in the churches of the so-called developed nations, the kind of churches people rarely write books about—who do not have a basic map of that faith which they believe links them with the Lord of eternal life. As they grow older, the detached ideas floating around in their minds easily mix with the prevailing folklore that they pick up from religious and unbelieving people alike, and their own brand of theology develops along the lines of Mr Badger's 'common sense' dogmatics.

THE JIGSAW

Have you ever seen a double-sided jigsaw of a jigsaw—a thing with no picture on it, just the outline of another jigsaw printed on it, and the whole thing two-sided? A few years ago in the United States, my eyes lighted on such a thing and it looked almost as threatening as a live snake! Even if you're very good at jigsaws, and not many of us are, I think you might be tempted to give up after you've done the bit round the edge. And if your friends should pour scorn on your limited success, you would have every right to remind them how difficult it is to get the pieces the right way up, let alone to get them to fit together without any kind of picture to work from! You'd probably say (and so would I) that it's quite an achievement to put together 50 pieces of double-sided jigsaw of a jigsaw.

That's the kind of confusion of Christian thinking that we're facing now, because many modern churchgoers are receiving almost no help to put together the jigsaw of biblical theology, and, when they start barely knowing what they are trying to do, they feel quite content if they can put together a few pieces round the edges of belief. It is not really their fault: they need proper training in the faith in the first place, and consistent teaching after that, to help them in their own piecing-together of what God has revealed of himself and his world.

This failure to put together the jigsaw of primary Christian truth leads to confusion and disorientation. Many of the arch-heretics in the history of the Church have been people with a similarly partial picture of God. Indeed, many ordinary Christians who turn up for church Sunday by Sunday find that after years of this kind of confusion they begin to get muddled about even the most important aspects of our faith-relationship with God in Christ. That friendship with Christ, that intimate sense of the fatherhood of God, turns into a system of religion with all its striving for God's acceptance and favour. Andrew Kirk, in a recent reflection, notes that zealous observance of religion does not bring salvation.

> Religious observance—the attempt to establish a righteous life—is one thing; salvation—accepting God's free gift of forgiveness and new life, and demonstrating this in a transformed existence—is something wholly different... The preaching of grace and faith is a great scandal to the religious mind, for it is inevitably a negative judgement on the religious person's observance and traditions.[1]

In an age when the Church has unparalleled opportunities for evangelism, as the mass of people turns away from pointless things like possessions and money and success, the Church finds itself in an internal crisis. The people of Christ as we see them are, for the most part, barely conversant with the things they claim to believe.

We can see this in the current growth of home-based Christian groups, supplying a very important need for Christians to get together in reading and studying the Bible, praying and sharing one another's joys, sorrows and gifts. It may take an enormous step of courage to join one of these home-groups but, once part of the fellowship, the Christian begins to grow spiritually by the week; few fail to have taken enormous strides forward in Christian understanding and maturity after some months in such company. What those groups are doing (and thank God for them) shows up what we are failing to do in Christian worship and preaching. For we have not only failed to provide, through our worship, a coherent map of our faith, but we have failed to reach people's real needs and thus failed to come anywhere near to their springs of motivation.

Ian Bunting has written: 'We have preached a faith which

has barely touched upon the everyday lives of our people and has not fully reflected the scandalous intrusion of the incarnate Christ into our murky world.'[2] When our preaching does not meet real spiritual needs and fails to motivate people, a major consequence is that personal witness to Christ becomes inarticulate and eventually dries up, the desire to share in God's mission evaporates, and comfortable pew Christianity is established. That kind of fat cat religion is the opposite of the Gospel, and poison for the Church.

Certainly in my own Anglican tradition there is growing pressure to admit children to communion at ever-younger ages. It's not my place here to argue the rights and wrongs of that issue, except to note that if the only period of training we are giving to young people nurtured within the Christian family (that is, those who have acquired their faith as they grew up) is in their early teens, then we are almost certain to fail. What we are doing is showing mentally and spiritually immature young people how to do a plywood ten-piece puzzle and then leaving them with the double-sided jigsaw of a jigsaw to sort out for themselves. It is no wonder that many of them throw the jigsaw away in frustration or do what Mr Badger has done: give it up as impossible. Some of the answer to this problem must lie in better church membership training, and not just for teenagers but also for adults to rethink their faith in adult life, including those who have been warming the pews in our churches for generations. Yet it may well be that the weekly teaching ministry of the Christian preacher is even more important to the average churchgoer than appropriate and regular membership training. For the preacher should be seeking not just to set down the pieces of the jigsaw in some random order but to help his people (many of whom are scared of the thought of home-groups and think they don't need a refresher course) to put a few pieces together in the right places and to help them to help other people struggling with the jigsaw.

PLANNED PREACHING

In the New Testament there are three essential elements of Christian discipleship: evangelism, baptism and education.

> Jesus drew near and said to them, 'I have been given all authority in heaven and on earth. Go, then, to all peoples everywhere and make them my disciples: baptize them in the name of the Father, the Son, and the Holy Spirit, and teach them to obey everything I have commanded you. And I will be with you always, to the end of the age.'   (Matthew 28:18–20)

Evangelism is the preaching and the sharing of the Good News of Jesus Christ leading to repentance and to faith. *Baptism* into the Church, the body of Jesus Christ, speaks of our redemption and our welcome into the family of God. *Education* in the truths and practices of the Christian faith, based upon what God has revealed, leads to a life of obedience.

In the first generation of the Christian Church, as Luke's account in The Acts of the Apostles demonstrates, when conversion was the order of the day and nurture almost unknown because not yet necessary, the pattern was simply the one recorded by Matthew: evangelism, baptism and education, each of them being taken seriously. And in many places for many people the pattern is still the same today. However, as one generation followed another, the practice of infant baptism followed by nurture, combining education with evangelism—became the norm; or sometimes, the pattern was evangelism, education and baptism—there have been many variations of these essential elements throughout the Church's history. Of one thing we can be certain: education is an important part of this pattern. Until we realise that passing on a few bits and pieces of the faith to the next generation and leaving it to them to sort it out is not what Jesus intended, we shall never convince many

Christians of the need for consistent preaching.

It is not simply that separate individuals need the benefit of planned preaching but also that such preaching is vital to the Church's mission and witness. Of course, it is very important that when Christians are engaged in sharing their faith with other people, they should be able to speak of their own experience of Christ, to tell their own story, but they will also need to tell the unchanging story of the Gospel and to be able to put it into words which their friends can understand. We rejoice when God takes hold of a person's spirit and directs his will: such a person has an enormous amount to offer to his friends as he shares with them the Good News of Christ. Yet his *mind* must also be captivated by God. And just as God does not emaciate the spirit and the will of a human being when he takes control of that person's life, so he does not turn that Christian into a gibbering fool! He longs for all who love him to give their minds to him and to use their minds in his service. In contrast, week after week in so many places, a mindless brand of Christianity is served up from the pulpit.

Sermons have been very important in the worship of the people of God since the earliest times. Using our broad definition of preaching, God's instruction to Adam and Eve not to touch the fruit of the tree in the middle of the garden might have been the first sermon, though the text is not recorded! From the time of the family of Abraham, there is a clear implication that God expects his people to be nurtured from generation to generation in faith and truth. And, by the time we reach the story of Moses and the Exodus from Egypt, the wanderings in the wilderness and the approach to the Promised Land, the people are specifically instructed to give priority to nurturing the faith and practice of the old covenant and the law.

Though the 'gathered church' practice of the synagogue did not develop until many centuries after Moses at the time of the exile in Babylonia, it is certain that in the latter period of the Old Testament and in the time of our Lord Jesus' earthly ministry, the synagogue was the most important regular religious influence on the life of God's ordinary people. And one of the most important parts of synagogue worship, then as now, is the reading and exposition of the Scriptures. It is that pattern of the old synagogue, combined with the impelling power of the Holy Spirit to share the Good News, which made preaching such an important part of the internal and external life of the Christian Church from the beginning.

Dietrich Bonhoeffer[3] was, I am sure, writing of the whole history of the Church when he envisaged 'Christ entering the congregation' through biblical preaching, dealing with our problem of sin by offering us the way of forgiveness, answering our searching for God by showing us himself, providing for our need and weakness by calling us to accept God's resources, and relieving our confusion by gently guiding us into the future. If preaching is, as I hope you believe it to be, as important as this, it is no wonder that our neglect of it as preachers and hearers has led to our spiritual poverty. John Donne (1572–1631) wrote of the honour of preaching:

> What a coronation is our taking of orders, and what inthronization is the coming up into the pulpit, where God invests his servants with his ordinance... 'Woe be unto thee if thou do not preach', and then enables him to preach peace, mercy, consolation, to the whole congregation.[4]

And that priestly honour of preaching has been no less regarded by some in our own century. As Bishop Hensley Henson wrote in 1927: 'Of all the actions of the Christian ministry preaching is the highest, and the test of our reverence for our profession is our performance of the preacher's duty.'[5]

During a number of troubles in some British cities in recent years, we've heard commentators on television and radio talk about 'no-go areas' for the police. There have also been some no-go areas for preachers. The Sunday morning 'early Communion' popular among some Christians in certain traditions has often been regarded as a no-go area!

My knowledge of Christians who value services like this (at which there has often been no preaching) has consistently led me to the discovery of two very different types of person in the congregation. One is a person very deeply committed to his Lord and equally committed to the Church and to the great truths of the Christian faith; he values the quieter nature of the early morning service for God to calm his frenzied activity of the previous week and to focus his mind and heart and will on the Lord for worship and service later in the day. The other is too often, sadly, one whose faith is never shared and therefore secret; whose knowledge of Christian things is remarkably limited and usually a soup of childhood memories mixed with the effects of television hymn-singing programmes! With the care for this second group of people as a priority, it is the preacher's duty not to remain silent, though he or she will want to be more reflective on those occasions.

In thinking about preaching (by which he meant all kinds of Christian witness), Karl Barth, one of the most significant theologians of this century, saw a comparison with the sacraments. The humble loaf and cup of wine become vehicles by which we come into special communion with God in Christ; so the humble words of Christian preaching are the means through which God speaks to human beings in every age, and that is because the Christian Church has been commissioned for this task by God himself.

How are we, then, to provide consistent preaching from week to week? Many people find the answer to this in using some kind of lectionary, a diary of Bible readings for each day of the year or at least for each Sunday. Lectionaries are not new: they were used in the Old Testament synagogues. There are basically two kinds available today. One provides each Sunday of the year with sets of readings on some particular theme—for instance, readings to do with the nature of the Bible on the second Sunday in the season of Advent. This thematic type of lectionary usually runs out of steam if extended over more than a two-year cycle, so that is its limit. There are also some thematic lectionaries that run on a mere one-year cycle, but these seriously neglect a large compass of Scripture.

It is, of course, valuable to have all the readings in one act of worship selected to teach different aspects of one theme; the preacher can refer with ease to the three or four readings already heard, and that will make it easier for him to perform one-off masterpieces! But we have noted that the more serious problem is long-term consistency, and the preacher will find his people not so well-fed after a few years of this thematic approach to Bible reading. They may be a good deal less disoriented than they would be if they were left simply to the mercies of the parson's whim, but they will not know the experience of following through a book of the Bible from week to week with sufficient consistency to begin to understand it at a deeper level.

The other type of lectionary seeks to read through a larger number of biblical books consecutively, providing more continuity from one week to the next, without necessarily providing a linking theme for each Sunday. This is in fact a much more traditional way of going about the reading of the Scriptures and is less vulnerable to the bias of the com-pilers. The current Roman Catholic three-year cycle of read-ings, based on reading almost all of the Gospels with large chunks of the Old Testament and most of the New, has been widely taken up among Protestant Christians worldwide, with some minor adjustments. When it comes to putting together the biblical jigsaw, I'm certain that it's more use to put together a few pieces from one area of the whole than to be assured that several pieces from all over the jigsaw are similarly theme-shaped! However, most of us who belong to churches that use lectionaries do not have much freedom to choose. The situation is even more serious for those few churches which still have inadequate lectionary patterns: reading even less of the Bible than if it were a *Reader's Digest* condensed book.

I have hinted at something worse than a bad lectionary: the tyranny of the preacher who, week by week, fumbles around for something to say and ends up giving you his thoughts on the current dispute in some branch of industry, or his trivial reflections on the international scene, or some other meddling in subjects which he and some of his people may find very interesting, but in which he is not called to be expert. Sermons which rely for most of their inspiration on the news can so easily become just an exercise in religious journalism; 'flabby platitudes', wrote B L Manning in 1939, that critical year in the world's history, 'about the dangers of the international situation, or the benevolent common-places of Ella Wheeler Wilcox expressed even more prosai-cally than in her poetry.'[6] The thought of such a preacher always reminds me of my fading memory of a Giles cartoon of the Sunflower League in some obscure village passing a resolution to ask Mr Kruschov to dismantle the Iron Cur-tain as long as he doesn't sell it to Herr Krupps to make bul-lets!

Having a good lectionary available to the preacher is part of the answer to the problem of biblical confusion in our churches. I suppose it's true that, for the nation, beer is no longer our common drink; more and more people have taken to making and sipping wine. One of the problems of any selection of passages from the Scriptures is the sipping of extracts that are too small, which jump in halfway through the writer's train of thought and hop out again before it's finished. In our churches we have laid less emphasis on the importance of reading and listening to a proper draught of biblical ale and have replaced it with some polite sips.

Whether or not a preacher has a lectionary at his disposal, he or she should always plan ahead, and those who listen to sermons should insist that he does. Some years ago, I devised my own four-year pattern of preaching which aimed to cover a large scope of the sort of things Christians believe and do. It sought to approach all the biblical books, themes and personalities, fitting into the mood of the Church's year from Advent to Christmas, Lent and Passiontide to Easter, Pentecost and Thanksgiving; it left some scope to look at the lives of a few great Christians, to examine some important moral issues, to deepen our life of prayer and so on. Even so, it was very selective, and a few years later I expanded it to a five-year pattern which, by the time we have responded to special needs and occasions, will, in fact, take about six years to work through. I'm certainly not alone in having developed a scheme like this, and I have no intention of putting it down in writing for others to copy, because it's important that preachers should do this for themselves and should also know when to set it aside.

In developing a long-term pattern for preaching, it is important to deal not only with biblical books but also with critical moral and doctrinal questions facing today's disciples. I recall John Stott saying that 'If we banish from the pulpit those topics which are most relevant in the world, it is not surprising that our people wonder if our preaching is relevant to their lives',[7] and Phillips Brooks' *Lectures on Preaching* in 1877 included this important call:

> The preachers that have moved and held men have always preached doctrine. No exhortation to good life that does not put behind it some truth as deep as eternity can seize and hold the conscience. Preach doctrine, preach all the doctrine that you know, and learn forever more and more; but preach it always not that men may believe it, but that men may be saved by believing it.[8]

I hope I have put a realistic case for systematic preaching, yet some preachers become so hooked that they begin to over-preach a book or a theme. I would not be surprised if you could take me into a Christian bookshop near your home and show me a wall of cassettes of some well-known preacher's sacred utterances on the New Testament or even, perhaps, just one book of it. Sadly, such idolatry is not as rare as it should be, as though any one servant of Jesus Christ, however gifted, could give you the definitive interpretation of Romans, let us say, for all time! Most of the best sermons are fresh food and therefore perishable. The Scriptures themselves are constantly being refreshed by God as we read them, hear them, share them and obey them.

It needs also to be said clearly that good preaching in churches is to be encouraged primarily for the benefit of those who are there already, so that they will be informed, inspired and motivated to engage in God's mission to the world. Some of the mostly deeply committed Christians I have come across, including those who take very seriously their own witness to Christ in daily living, have told me that they're 'working on Arthur and Amanda to get them to church' so they hope it will be a decent sermon on that day—not always a certainty by any means when I'm preaching! But the Church is not a cafeteria to which we bring people for feeding on the dish they think looks the tastiest. It should not be a eucharistic cafeteria, with as many Communions in one day as there are divisions of opinion as to how and when the Lord's Supper should be celebrated, for that is to deny the uniting nature of the sacrament; nor should it be a preaching cafeteria, with pulpit-calls constantly served up to meet the needs of visitors and the unconverted, for that is, over a period of time, to cause spiritual indigestion. The worship of the people of God each week, a sharing in the heavenly banquet rather than a trip to a religious burger bar for a quarterpounder of spiritual meat in a bread-of-life bun, may well have converting power of itself but it is not the primary vehicle for evangelism. Evangelism—the shouting of the Good News, the sharing of the gladness of Christ—is the job of the Church *outside* the walls of its building. If you ever persevere to the last chapter of this book, we'll return to this theme then.

The preacher can easily fall into the trap of speaking evangelistically all the time; it is often very successful and much admired by those who become totally dependent on the sermon to rekindle the fires of divine love within them. Most parsons know that when they preach an evangelistic sermon they will receive the warmest thanks from those in their congregation who are already committed Christians and who simply enjoyed the warm-up! And why shouldn't they have an occasional warm-up?—but not all the time. The pastor-preacher, the one who is committed to the local church in which he is called to speak, must be aware of the temptation to become simply an evangelist, for if he does not resist that temptation he will eventually produce people who leave their evangelism to him. Once that habit takes root, the Church as a body begins to retreat from its mission in the world, especially its mission to relations, friends, neighbours, workmates and so on.

It is often simply a confusion of terms: what we call 'preaching' is actually much closer to the work of teaching and nurture. What we call 'evangelism' is the corporate work of the Church in telling the Good News of Christ so that those who do not believe may receive life in union with him. When all our pulpit-preaching is evangelism, we can produce a numerically successful church, but we will have built it on shaky foundations. All this is not to say that there is no scope for the gospel in regular teaching sermons. It is a strange Christian preacher who does not make some reference to the gospel during each sermon as he preaches Christ, for Christ is the heart of the gospel.

I hope we will see that Mr Badger's blindspot is a problem which can be remedied by better and regular training in the essentials of our faith and by more systematic preaching.

One area remains: the pressure on the preacher. As the Church continues to develop in every-member ministry (for which we all thank God) and becomes less dependent on its professional ministry, those same ministers have to accept the rôle of co-ordinator for the local church's ministry, in addition to fulfilling the existing and powerful expectations of their congregations. And, because they so often feel obliged to meet even unreasonable expectations, the time they spend in preparation, not least in sermon preparation, is cut short. This may be because they have come to believe in the ineffectiveness of their preaching, or simply because they reckon that in the pulpit they can rely on their native wit or the constant grace of the Holy Spirit to make up for their constant failures

Back in 1939 (before the so-called numerical crisis in the Christian ministry overtook us) Charles Smyth commented:

> You may say that the real trouble is that we are most of us too overworked and too shorthanded, too much engaged in serving tables, to have time to compose fine sermons. That is true: but, in the first place, nobody wants fine sermons—fine sermons are one of the most dangerous of the Devil's snares: and in the second place, a knowledge of the rules of preaching, like a knowledge of the multiplication table or of the rudiments of first aid, would save an infinity of time and trouble and of aimless fumbling.[9]

Back in the Acts of the Apostles, they recognised that the preacher had to be given time for his work (Acts 6:1–6) and 'ordained' six people for work as deacons in order to relieve the pressure on the preachers.

I asked a friend of mine who is vicar of an inner-city parish when he found time to prepare sermons in that most demanding ministry. He told me that he goes to a quiet corner of the church about forty minutes before worship: he spends some time in prayer and silence, some time in reading and thinking, then he makes a few notes and it's time to get other things ready for worship. I've no doubt he's right that sermons have to be heard coming from the preacher's heart if they are to reach people's hearts and wills, though I would need to be better prepared if I were in his place. Well over a century ago, Bishop Samuel Wilberforce ('Soapy Sam' as they called him because of his ready eloquence) noted that 'Some clergy prepare their sermons; others prepare themselves.' No doubt he, too, was right in emphasising the preacher's preparation of his own soul. But that must never excuse a failure to do one's homework.

NOTES

1   Andrew Kirk, 'The Middle East Dilemma. A Personal Reflection', *Anvil* vol 3, no 3, (1986): p 251.
2   I D Bunting, *Preaching at Communion (i)* (Grove: Nottingham, 1981), p 7.
3   Dietrich Bonhoeffer, *The Cost of Discipleship* (SCM: London, 1959), p 225.
4   E M Simpson and G R Potter, ed. *The Sermons of John Donne* (University of California: 1954), vol 7, sermon dated 18 April 1626, pp 118–140.
5   Hensley Henson, *Church and Parson in England* (Hodder and Stoughton: London, 1927), p 153.
6   B L Manning, *Essays in Orthodox Dissent* (1939), p 61.
7   A live quotation from John Stott in Saint Mark's Church, Cardiff, November 1985
8   Phillips Brooks, *Lectures on Preaching, 1877* (Allinson: London, 1895), p 129.
9   Charles Smyth, *The Art of Preaching, 747–1939* (SPCK: London, 1940), p 2.

Chapter 3

HE NEEDS A DECENT WATCH:
Alfred Downspout's Lunch

Mr Alfred Downspout never eats much breakfast, at least not since he retired from work, but he does enjoy a decent lunch, and particularly a good Sunday lunch. He usually sets off from home at about half past ten on a Sunday and takes a stroll through the park on his way to church, so that he arrives in a quiet frame of mind, ready for the sort of service that doesn't disturb him too much. He likes things to be as they've always been: the same things in the same places—he knows every stone in the church building; the same people in the same pews; the same kind of service; and the same kind of hymns he's known since childhood. He's even got used to the well-worn Bible readings and the same kind of sermons for the various seasons of the year. In fact, he'd probably heard every one of the old vicar's sermons several times over. That was the comforting thing about the old vicar, you could set your watch by his sermons, always around twelve minutes. Alfred didn't much need a watch when he was in church because, as every seasoned sermon-taster knows, a twelve-minute sermon is about as long as it takes to suck a large pear drop. When the old vicar said, 'In conclusion, my dear brethren,' he did conclude. Even when Mr Grind, the lay reader, says, 'Finally, friends,' it isn't long before he finishes. But this new man, the Reverend Septimus Snuffle, when he says, 'Lastly, everyone,' he certainly can make it last! He needs a decent watch!

Take last Sunday for example. The vicar had hardly got into his stride before Mr Downspout had finished his pear drop and it took four more extra-strong mints before the vicar eventually dried up, though, when Alfred protested loudly to his friends about this (out of the vicar's earshot) he forgot to mention that he'd crunched the last mint because he was so annoyed—and crunching sermon-sweets is quite contrary to the rules of this game! His wife was expecting him home for lunch soon after twelve o'clock, but last Sunday it was nearly half past when he came rushing up the garden path in a frightful lather, puffing and blowing and letting off some very incoherent steam about modern vicars and long sermons and a new hymn and something about children, and who'd moved the umbrella stand? Well, he was well into his main course of roast beef and Yorkshire pudding before he'd calmed down enough to blame the vicar for the fact that his wife had rather overcooked the meat! 'All this for a sermon!', he kept muttering under his breath (Mrs Downspout having forbidden him to go on any longer about it), and eventually he came to the conclusion that he'd have to stop going every week if the vicar was going to go on like that. It has to be admitted that Parson Snuffle is not without blame in this matter: he does tend to rabbit on about things which haven't much to do with the theme of his sermon. But Mr Downspout's got a problem: he doesn't really want to hear the word of God if it takes more than twelve minutes or spoils his Sunday lunch.

Short sermons are the order of the day in many of the world's Western (or Northern) churches, and it is time that the tyranny of the short sermon should be challenged. It is not that short sermons are always wrong, but that they are not always right. The saying that 'sermonettes breed Christianettes' (variously attributed to several famous preachers in this century) ought to be taken more seriously.

One of the most delightful characters to appear out of the late eighteenth and early nineteenth centuries is William Farish, for forty years vicar of Saint Giles' Church in Cambridge and professor first of chemistry, then of natural philosophy. Farish must have been the model for the absent-minded professor, branded as being of unsound mind because he told a parliamentary committee that trains might one day run at 60 miles an hour, and known to have boiled his watch while timing it with an egg he held in his hand!

Legend has it that Farish, about to travel on horseback to conduct a service in some outlying church, mounted his horse on one side, surveyed the world for a moment and then dismounted on the other side, assuming that he had already arrived at his destination. The scene is comic, but if ever you have suffered from a lapse of memory and can't remember doing something you know you must have done, you may also have some sympathy. Without condemning every short sermon (for that is certainly not my intention) I have a good idea that most of them are rather like Farish's horse-ride: the preacher hops on to one side of his text, sits there for a minute taking a look at the world around, and then hops off again, quite delighted that he has reached his intended destination. His bemused congregation soon gets into the habit of applauding this liturgical joke and takes to condemning preachers who spend time travelling somewhere on their sermons, so badly encroaching on the time for lunch.

BOREDOM

So let's try to discover what it is that makes people bored when they listen to sermons. I'd like to suggest six causes for the onset of boredom.

The first cause of boredom is the possibility that the preacher himself is bored. Some people assume that preachers are immune to the kind of temptations to which the rest of humanity is prey. No matter how real he or she may seem to be, ordination is conceived by the person in the pew to have raised the preacher out of the way of so many ordinary temptations—to doubt, to the cooling of his love for God or to a sense of despondency. When a priest or minister or lay preacher is found to have committed some sin on which society enjoys frowning, the stock criticism is that 'he has betrayed the trust placed in him'. But deeper down is the feeling among people inside and outside the

Church that the man's ordination should have immunised him from ordinary people's temptations; for this servant of God to have fallen, he must have been very weak and vulnerable in the first place—a good excuse for the newspapers to kick him about a bit!

I have no doubt that the moral and spiritual standards of the clergy in all traditions of the Christian Church today are as good as those of their people, but congregations must be aware of the temptations to depression, despondency and even disbelief which come to their ministers as to them. At times like those, thankfully short-lived for most of us, it can be very hard to preach.

There may even be times when a whole community is devastated by some disaster—I think of that appalling tragedy at Aberfan in South Wales in 1966 when nearly half a generation of schoolchildren and many of their teachers died as a slag-heap slipped and engulfed their school. No doubt almost every preacher in the country referred to that tragic incident on the following Sunday, and if anyone did so without a sense of holy disbelief, he must have been a hard man, or one unwilling to remove the mask—perhaps even when he looked in the mirror. And the same reaction could be true of the news we hear of starvation, disease and war in so many parts of the world. There is a time when it is right for a preacher to be stunned into silence with his people. To mouth slick words on occasions like these is to create more revulsion than boredom.

Yet in the normal course of our experience, preachers cannot claim that kind of excuse. The simple fact is that many preachers have become bored with the story they have been commissioned to tell. It is said that an Archbishop of Canterbury—I think it was John Tillotson—asked Thomas Betterton, the actor, why he thought that so many preachers left their congregations unmoved, whereas actors stirred the feelings of their audiences. Betterton is said to have replied, 'Actors speak of things imaginary as if they were real, but you preachers too often speak of things real as if they were imaginary.'[1] It may simply be a problem of delivery, with a preacher rushing through a very full script, barely taking time to look up at the light-fittings in between outpourings of theology. Or it may be quite simply that if the preacher has no fire of love for the Lord in his heart, he is unlikely to set anyone else on fire with his message. But even boredom can be redeemed. I recall a comment made by a wise man to a group of his colleagues in the ministry: 'If you as a preacher sometimes feel bored, that's no bad thing. God may want you to be bored in order to help you understand what it's like to listen to one of your own sermons.'

The second cause for boredom is a basic spiritual fact: God does not expect his message to be popular. Do you recall, when Isaiah was called to the prophetic ministry, what God said to him? Some of us have Isaiah 6:1–8 imprinted on our minds from its regular appearance at school assembly in order to remind us of the great British virtues of sacrifice and service, but the reading never went on beyond verse eight. You remember how it ended: 'Then I heard the Lord say, "Whom shall I send? Who will be our messenger?" I answered, "I will go! Send me!"' (v 8). But the text goes on:

> So he told me to go and give the people this message: 'No matter how much you listen, you will not understand. No matter how much you look, you will not know what is happening.' Then he said to me, 'Make the minds of these people dull, their ears deaf, and their eyes blind, so that they cannot see or hear or understand. If they did they might turn to me and be healed.'
>
> (Isaiah 8:9–10)

Or do you remember the call of Jeremiah recounted in the first chapter of his prophecies, when God calls this very young man with such a sense of divine authority, but has to assure the prophet that he will not leave him in his future struggle?

Get ready, Jeremiah; go and tell them everything I command you to say. Do not be afraid of them now, or I will make you even more afraid when you are with them. Listen, Jeremiah! Everyone in this land—the kings of Judah, the officials, the priests and the people—will be against you. But today I am giving you the strength to resist them; you will be like a fortified city, an iron pillar, and a bronze wall. They will not defeat you, for I will be with you to protect you. I, the LORD, have spoken. (Jeremiah 1:17–19)

Jeremiah's ministry was marked by a singular lack of 'success' in the popular sense of the word, and he openly complains to the Lord in face of priestly opposition, a complaint which has been such an encouragement to preachers over the years.

> LORD, you have deceived me,
>   and I was deceived.
> You are stronger than I am,
>   and you have overpowered me.
> Everyone jeers at me;
>   they mock me all day long.
> Whenever I speak, I have to cry out
>   and shout, 'Violence! Destruction!'
> LORD, I am ridiculed and scorned all the time,
>   because I proclaim your message.
> But when I say, 'I will forget the LORD
>   and no longer speak in his name,'
> then your message is like a fire
>   burning deep within me.
> I try my best to hold it in,
>   but can no longer keep it back.' (Jeremiah 20:7–9)

This is something for those who do *not* preach sermons to take to heart, rather than a ready-made excuse for a failing preacher. You will, no doubt, have heard a certain type of Christian explain why some particular church is full for all services every Sunday: 'It's because they preach the Gospel there.' In a different circumstance, the very same pietist can be heard explaining why so few people attend another church: 'It's because they preach the Gospel there.' Popular success, or failure, is a very poor guide to truth. Do you recall the prayer of Ignatius of Loyola (1491–1556): 'Teach us, good Lord, ... to labour and not to ask for any reward, save that of knowing that we do your will'?

The third cause of boredom with sermons is feeble content. If sermons are trivial or irrelevant or lacking in the scope of eternity, they will become tiresome to hear. Gerhard Ebeling has written, 'What an expenditure of effort is put into the preaching of the Christian faith up and down the land! But—again with exceptions—is it not the institutionally assured platitudes which are preached?'[2]

Many preachers have taken to giving advice on how to cure the symptoms of the human predicament, how to deal with a sin here and a sin there. This would be a nice way of coping with spiritual hypochondriacs, but most people in our churches do not have imaginary spiritual problems, nor can their problems be cured by a dose of some comforting but ineffective placebo: 'When, my friends, is a white lie not an untruth?', or 'How we should deal with the problem of greed?', or (usually to a congregation whose age makes the issue almost meaningless) 'How to solve our problem of lust'. All these might be the right questions to deal with in smaller contexts and with particular groups of people but generally the preacher must tackle principles of far greater importance: the eternal matter of our relationship with God in Christ, and our consequent relationships with one another. The story is told of a confirmation service at Sherborne School at the turn of the century, during which Bishop John Wordsworth 'vehemently implored the boys, whatever else they might do, on no account to marry their Deceased Wives' Sisters.'[3]

Too many preachers do a kind of homiletic striptease in the pulpit as they spend a quarter of an hour uncovering their souls and exposing all their sins in the name of trying to help their people, whose only interest in the sermon is what their pastor is revealing about his inner life! Joseph Parker (1830–1902), one of the masters of the nineteenth century pulpit, once asked an aspiring preacher to deliver his best sermon. Afterwards the great man commented, 'For the last half hour you have not been trying to get something into my mind but something off yours. You are like a man anxious to get rid of a sack of coals.'[4] A good sermon, then, enables the living word in the Scriptures to meet each human being in his need and to introduce him to Jesus Christ. Thus the issues with which the preacher deals are the eternal ones of God and humanity, revealed in the Bible.

Of course, those issues must meet human beings where they are, and therefore they must be related to real human experiences in the place and at the time in which the preacher speaks. I have the profoundest respect for the word of God in the whole of the Scriptures, including the tricky 613 commands of the Torah, the ritual and moral details of God's law in the Old Covenant, but I doubt whether a series of sermons on each of these 613 commands, no matter how well related to the revelation in Christ, would be especially helpful to the average congregation today—and I guess the preacher would have to labour his points very strenuously in the process. It is the duty of a preacher not only to bring the word of God to the people but also to bring the people and their needs to the word of God.

I heard of a preacher at a family service who had struggled for 28 minutes on a children's talk about the parable of the wheat and the weeds (Matthew 13:24–30), and at the end asked the weary congregation to tell him something from his text. The children were silent, so he foolishly asked the adults. One wise old Christian, familiar with the King James version of the Bible, shouted out: 'O Timothy, avoid profane and vain babblings'! (I Timothy 6:20 and II Timothy 2:16).

The fourth cause of boredom in preaching is that few people outside academic circles (except Garrison Keillor fans) listen to long monologues these days. We can, therefore, too easily ignore this fact and exaggerate the case for the sermon. No doubt this is done out of the purest of motives and respect for this ancient tradition and for the real value which is gained from it by the people of God. However, I think there may be an underlying reluctance to accept and implement change in the case that is made for the *total dominance* of the solo sermon, even among people with little resemblance to Alfred Downspout. Sometimes the case is made strongly by those 'giants' among God's servants to whom thousands of people come to hear God's word in their preaching: it would be astonishing to hear anything other than a stout defence of the pulpit from them. The pressures of time also conspire against the frequent use of alternatives to the preacher in the pulpit. We may well think that it is appropriate and right to introduce alternative methods of communication, ancient and modern, to replace the ministry of the pulpit from time to time, but the necessary preparation involved for almost any alternative is considerably greater and involves more people than that required for the preparation of a sermon. We must be agreed that, as a normal practice, the monologue sermon is with us to stay.

There are those who argue that, since there is no regular alternative to orthodox preaching, it is necessary to cut down the amount of time that is spent in the pulpit because people cannot listen attentively for more than a short period of time. It is quite true that performances of opera or of the plays of Shakespeare on television can be quite tedious, even to those who would find them most exciting and stimulating in the live theatre. Even pop music has to be dished up with more and more extravagant visual techniques on television and video to attract the attention of its admirers. News programmes on television are cut up into easily-digestible units: snappy one-liners at the beginning between dramatic bursts of theme music, followed by individual reports lasting usually no more than three or four minutes, and concluding with a summary of the main items of the news and the funny story of the day. In the face of this, it is said that normal people cannot listen for 20 minutes or even half an hour to one person speaking without being bored out of their minds. And the conclusion that is drawn is that the monologue technique is no way to present the Christian gospel.

Some of the best of the long-sermon preachers would not disagree. A tedious monologue lasting only a few minutes can seem like half a lifetime when you're longing for it to finish! It is told that a minister who thought very highly of his gift as a preacher became more and more distraught as, week after week, he noticed Mrs Jones closing her eyes as he began his oration and not opening them again until the following hymn. At last his frustration got the better of him and he asked her, as nicely as he could, why she always went to sleep during his sermons. 'Oh my dear, I'm not sleeping,' she replied; 'I just find it easier to work out tomorrow's shopping list with my eyes closed.' Mrs Jones may not be able to concentrate on her shopping list, let alone a sermon, and Mr Downspout will have trouble from his dentist because of all the sweets he's getting through during those long orations, but it is nevertheless a fact that Christian people *can* listen attentively to a 30-minute sermon regularly without rigor mortis setting in. For all the fair arguments raised against extended monologue preaching, it is simply not true to say that it has no power or effectiveness in this latter part of the twentieth century. That's what this book is setting out to show!

There are of course reasonable bounds to all preaching. Charles Simeon (1759–1836) advised the students who passed through his care: 'Never weary your hearers by long preaching', and 'endeavour to rivet their attention on your message for a reasonable time; but remember, that the mind, and especially among the generality of persons or the uneducated, will only bear a certain amount of tension.'[5] Despite that warning, Simeon preached regularly for fifty minutes. John Stott, a preacher not normally characterised by undue brevity or tedium, in his magnificent book, *I Believe in Preaching*, confided,

> I think every sermon should last just as long as the preacher needs in which to deliver his soul. Basically, it is not the length of a sermon which makes the congregation impatient for it to stop, but the tedium of a sermon in which even the preacher himself appears to be taking very little interest.[6]

And he concludes with a tentative rule of thumb that 'ten minutes are too short and forty minutes too long'. It has been wisely said that every sermon should 'seem like twenty minutes', even if it is actually longer.'[7] P T Forsyth also commented:

> ... in my humble judgment the demand for short sermons on the part of Christian people is one of the most fatal influences to destroy preaching in the true sense of the word... Brevity may be the soul of wit, but the preacher is not a wit. And those who say they want little sermons because they are there to worship God and not to hear man, have not grasped the rudiments of the first idea of Christian worship... A Christianity of short sermons is a Christianity of short fibre.[8]

The fifth cause of boredom is faulty construction. What is said may be very sound and helpful, but the logical pattern is disrupted by a muddled presentation, or by a key fact in a story left out. Preaching is not simply the piling of facts on top of one another, like building blocks in a nursery; not simply an exercise in education; its pattern must be carefully designed for motivation as well as education. 'A sermon,' wrote H H Farmer, 'should have something of the quality of a knock on the door.'[9]

The preacher needs to cultivate a clear mind, capable of looking at the world like any other person without necessarily coming to the same conclusion. Thus the preacher looks at life as Miss Marple looked at one of those crimes created for her by Agatha Christie, able to distinguish the things that matter in the mystery of life from the flamboyant irrelevancies to which we usually pay undue attention. This is an important attitude for observing the work of God in our daily life and experience. The logic of the preacher's thinking must also be clear, drawn from the subject being examined—usually some biblical text or passage. This may well mean sorting the ideas into a different pattern from the original, in order to produce an exposition which is not only faithful to it but also intelligible. There must also be some clarity—'transparency' is, I think, the current word for it—in the overall pattern and shape of the sermon, so that, whether or not the preacher 'tells 'em he's going to tell 'em, tells 'em, and then tells 'em he's told 'em' or not, the congregation still knows where he's going. There is a fine balance here between having a clear shape to a sermon, and saying so much towards the beginning of it that the remaining time feels like padding. It does not really matter whether the preacher lets the congregation into the secret of his sermon's shape near the beginning; what matters, if they are not to become bored, is that there should be some element of surprise and revelation throughout its length. Even the type of sermon which has no division into several points can have a shape, as a story is carefully told and a window opened on another view of the love of God.

The sixth cause of boredom among congregations is a lack of variety in the preacher's technique. There used to be a theory that the Christian minister, in leading worship and preaching, should seek to remain as dispassionate as possible, to be detached, not emotionally involved, not carried away by his message, so that he could not be accused of using worldly tricks to produce Christians. The underlying notion of not using worldly tricks to con people into Christian faith is at least as old as Saint Paul, and I'm sure we ought to take it more seriously than we do, but the poker-faced, monotonous drone of a tedious parson reading his notes as though they were a *Times* leader, has very little to do with Christian preaching.

There are some preachers who frown on humour in the pulpit—my problem is rather the reverse because I find it very difficult not to see the funny side of a lot of things, even things which I take very seriously. Without encouraging silly frivolity in the pulpit, there seems to me to be no reason why the Christian preacher cannot use God's gift of humour to aid him in his task; it can sometimes say far more than pages of serious words, and often it can create a mental image of the theme with which the preacher is dealing. I cannot imagine that all the parables of Jesus were told in a serious tone of voice—I guess there were some smiles as he told the story of the Pharisee praying in the front pew of the temple (Luke 18:9–14); and surely there were tears and smiles as the lost son returned to his father, and not a little wistful mirth at the proud reaction of his elder brother (Luke 15:11–32)

VARIETY

There is in the possession of the Church Pastoral-Aid Society a series of six silhouettes of Charles Simeon, drawn by Augustin Edouart in 1828, showing the preacher in a variety of postures. He leans forward, counting with the fingers of both hands, *expounding*; he holds his spectacles to his nose and peers down at his finger pointing to a biblical text, *acquiring*; he stands back, one arm gently reaching out to his hearers, *imparting*; he lifts his arms in a gesture of welcome and worship, *entreating*; he puts himself into a position of intercession with his people, *imploring*; and he stands back in an attitude of resignation, as though waiting for the people to make their own response, *concluding*.

Expounding

Imparting

Concluding

Entreating

Acquiring

Imploring

Charles Simeon, like so many great preachers before and since, knew the importance of variety within a sermon. Though taught in no theological college, but a student of the Holy Spirit and of human nature, I suspect that he would even have something to teach the sophisticated television communicators of our own age. A quick sketch of the techniques of a few Christian preachers over the years may help us to appreciate the need for variety and the development of preaching styles appropriate to the times in which we live.

As far back as the fourteenth century, Thomas Waleys (*De Modo Componendi Sermones cum Documentis*, about the year 1340), set out what is believed to have been a fairly standard mediaeval style, allegorised in the form of a tree. First, the preacher is to take the text—the root of the tree. Then he is to dangle a carrot to lead the donkeys of the congregation into the sermon: some kind of illustration leading to an invitation to pray—the trunk of the tree. The text is repeated for the benefit of latecomers (times haven't changed!), followed by the subject-matter in three phases of development—the branches of the tree. The fourth major section is the development of what has gone before, including an appeal to the hearers—the fruit and foliage of the tree. Thus, we should not dismiss mediaeval preachers, though, undoubtedly, Waleys represents a high-water mark in his tradition, since he insists that the tone of voice used by the preacher should be attractive, his pace of delivery should not be a gabble, his gestures should be natural, the length should be reasonable (encouraging preachers to stop before their hearers become restive!), and new preachers should practise their craft. So, he warns them of the seriousness of their high calling.

About a century later, the Franciscan preacher Bernardino of Siena (1380–1444) made his famous appeal for preaching in an age of sacramentalism:

And if of these two things you can do only one—either

hear the Mass or hear the sermon—you should let the Mass go, rather than the sermon... There is less peril for your soul in not hearing Mass than in not hearing the sermon.[10]

At much the same period, John Wyclif in England was insisting not just on longer texts for sermons (that is, on preaching from biblical passages and stories rather than from single phrases alone) but also that sermons should reveal to hearers 'the naked text', allowing the Bible to set the theme of the sermon. He despised both preaching to the gallery and preaching according to the formal niceties of his day. The 'Morning Star of the Reformation' was therefore not widely appreciated as a preacher by the people or by many of his fellow ecclesiastics.

The Reformation produced a number of great preachers, none more renowned than Bishop Hugh Latimer (1485–1555), whose sermons were both moving and memorable. The feature for which he should be most respected is his gift for moving from tangible things and human experiences to spiritual truths, as in his famous *Sermons on the Card* (the game of cards). Yet Thomas Birch's history of preaching, published in 1752, describes Latimer's sermons as 'defective in dignity and elegance, his frank remonstrances to persons of the highest rank being deliver'd in expressions of peculiar levity, and intermix'd with frequent stories unsuitable to the solemnity of the place or the occasions'![11]

The second and third generation of the Reformation produced, in England and Wales, men like the young Bishop John Jewel; and in Scotland, men like the fiery John Knox. Lancelot Andrewes (1555–1626) was probably a rather cool preacher but teaches us how important it is to have a careful pattern and division in a sermon. See him here splitting his texts like logs from Waleys' tree!

For all Texts come not asunder alike: For sometimes the Words naturally *fall asunder*; sometimes they *drop asunder*; sometimes they *melt*; sometimes they *untwist*; and there be some Words so willing to be parted, that they *divide themselves*, to the great ease and rejoicing of the Minister. But if they will not easily come in pieces, then he falls to hacking and hewing, as if he would make all fly in shivers. The Truth of it is, I have known, now and then, some knotty Texts, that have been divided seven or eight times over, before they could make them *split handsomely*, according to their mind.

But then comes the Joy of Joys, when the parts *jingle*, or begin with the same *Letter*...[12]

Following Andrewes, we could note the significant figure of John Donne (1572–1631), known in his early life as 'a great visitor of ladies', as his love poetry reveals, and ordained at the age of forty-three, becoming Dean of St Paul's six years later. His considerable learning in the Scriptures and the classics is evident in his sermons, which are sprinkled with biblical references and Latin tags. His style is far too dry for twentieth century taste, though his wit still shines through in places and, in his own time, he drew enormous congregations. Donne's sermons reveal a clear, analytical mind, combined with a mastery of English prose, yet they can never have the power over the human mind and heart that his Christian poetry commands.

Among other seventeenth-century preachers, we should not fail to note Richard Baxter (1615–1691) who followed up his lengthy preaching with detailed pastoral catechising. By the end of the seventeenth century, lively preaching was in the hands of the nonconformists and in the established Church a cooler, more rational and understated style was characterised by Archbishop John Tillotson. These were moral lessons thought suitable for the rational days of the Enlightenment: practical views of a God and a world capable of being grasped by the human intellect. These sermons did not seek to elicit any kind of response or answer, though they were copied by many of the parochial clergy, and Parson Woodforde, a century later, is a rural example of this school. Earthy Christians like Dr Samuel Johnson did not admire them.

Not all the world followed the rationalists, for some realised the need to preach to faith rather than to morality. There is a famous charge of Bishop Samuel Horsley (1733–1806) delivered in 1790 in which he accused such preaching of reducing 'practical Christianity to heathen virtue', contributing 'to divest our sermons of the genuine spirit and savour of Christianity, and to reduce them to mere moral essays', these things being 'quite out of their place in the pulpit'.[13]

He was by no means alone. Men after the spirit of John and Charles Wesley and of George Whitefield were, in contrast, profoundly convinced of the forgiving grace and redeeming love of God at work in their own lives and in the Church of their times. Although our own century is in many ways similar to that of the eighteenth, I don't think I would dare to do what John Wesley did in my own city of Cardiff in 1739, preaching for three hours in the open air. As they proclaimed the mystery of the Cross and of the Resurrection of Christ their appeal came through to thousands upon thousands of plain, unchurched people who found that the Spirit of God was at work in their lives. It is a serious indictment of the established Church that the Spirit-filled preaching of the Wesleys and the Methodists was driven out.

At the end of the eighteenth century and the beginning of the nineteenth, Charles Simeon realised the importance of teaching the art of preaching to the many Christian undergraduates who came within his sphere of influence and was probably the first preacher since the middle ages to teach it systematically. He himself was greatly indebted to the writings of Jean Claude (1618–1687), a French Reformed minister, for the basic principles underlying his preaching: urging a clear explanation of the entire text, simplicity, a lack of idle speculation, appealing to the hearts of the people, and not preaching to excess.

Generally, Simeon would announce a text and introduce its theme; he would provide the context and then divide the theme into several sections (five at most), each of which he would discuss before drawing some final conclusions, every conclusion being stronger than the one before it. It is fair to say that his weakness seems to have been a difficulty with illustration, but that is not surprising in one whom his friends described as lacking in aesthetic imagination! Simeon taught the churches the need for preacher-training.

The list of famous preachers in the nineteenth and early twentieth centuries could easily fill many pages, and each Christian tradition would be represented: the Free Churches, Roman Catholic and Anglican. The stream of evangelical preaching was in full spate, but it is my view that the emphasis in some places subtly shifted from God's appeal to the individual hearer, to the popular appeal of well-known preachers. If that is true, it may account for some of the loss of conviction among many local pastor-preachers in the last two generations.

HOW LONG IS A PIECE OF STRING?

Alfred Downspout still has to be convinced of the value of any sermon more than twelve minutes long! So how long should a sermon be? How long is a piece of string? There is an apocryphal story of the shortest sermon ever, preached, it is said, by Jonathan Swift (1667–1745) in aid of a charity. His text was: 'He that hath pity on the poor lendeth unto the LORD, and that which he hath given will he pay him again' (Proverbs 19:17). The sermon was a mere two sentences: 'Now, my friends, you hear the terms of the loan. If you like the security, down with the cash!'

There have also been sightings of daffodil-eating clergy whose brief sermons, presumably uttered a sentence at a time between munching at a floral display, have supposedly been about the Resurrection, but I have long since forgotten what the connection is! Last year I read that at least one of these annual oddities was taken ill before he reached the end of the service. At the other extreme is the Apostle Paul himself who, as Luke records in Acts 20:7–12, preached for so long in a confined space at Troas that Eutychus, a young member of his congregation, dropped off to sleep and fell out of the window!

There are really no rules as to the length of a sermon, but certain constraints are important in judging the right length for each sermon in each place at each time. In the first place, there will be the constraints of the place and the time of the sermon. A sermon preached in a fairly sophisticated congregation of mainly middle-class folk, many of whom have been well educated (the main breeding-ground of preachers, more's the pity) could be extended and ought to be relatively easy, providing the preacher does his homework. Another entirely different context is a small community, perhaps less than 20 people, who gather weekly in some secular building such as a school or a community hall or even a public house. There the preaching will have to be more direct, usually well planned extemporisation. In a rural setting there is a sense of intimacy already established, even with those who come occasionally, which the preacher can use to great effect in communication. Despite all the grouping of farms and mechanisation, the village preacher can still rely on an affinity between his people and the rural environment in which much of the Bible was written, and this should save him a lot of time and unnecessary explanation.

It may be that the time in which the worship takes place will constrain the style and length. I have already hinted that preaching at an early morning service requires a gentler, more meditative approach. Sometimes, if a minister has a large number of churches to care for, it may be that a service has to conclude within the space of 60 minutes. While it is a pity to put such restraints on worship, it is occasionally necessary, and, in that event, the preacher will have to decide on the correct balance for word, prayer and eucharist. But let him beware the trap of thinking, 'This service takes about 50 minutes, so that leaves 10 for the sermon.' That is *not* the way to obtain the correct balance in worship. If services have to be confined to short periods of time, it is wrong to sacrifice the sermon to the rest of the worship. A far better way is to recognise that their minister is not like an elastic band who can be stretched until he snaps—some local sharing of resources and fuller use of unordained Christian people in order to relieve the pressures of time are the proper answers.

A second major constraint on the length of sermons will be the people who listen to the sermon with whatever measure of biblical understanding among them and their capacity for listening. If I say that some congregations simply cannot take anything more than 15 minutes of eyeball-to-eyeball preaching, I am not insulting them; in fact, I often find a great deal of spiritual reality in just such places. Certain congregations, on the other hand, may simply have got into short sermon habits and the process of getting used to a new style can be painful, as Mr Downspout is beginning to discover. Donald Coggan has made the brave assertion, 'Better, far, to preach a little above their capacity than below it.'[14]

A final constraint is one on which the preacher must make a judgement while he is preaching: the response or 'feel' of the congregation to the words he is speaking. It may mean taking time to re-explain spontaneously when the congregation seems to be struggling to grasp a point, or it may mean cutting out a section if the people appear to have given up the struggle. Some advice along the lines of that given to junior lawyers is the only rule: 'If, after ten minutes, you do not strike oil, stop boring!' Knowing that it is time to abandon ship when you feel that sinking feeling is a hard but valuable lesson to learn.

There are a few rules which the preacher should take to heart if he wishes to remain on the point when he must be short and sharp. First, there should be a very concise pattern of thinking, with one theme in mind and one aim in view.

Second, any illustration must be precise, that is, in the right place and concise in its use of words. Third, the language used will depend on the context, but it must be appropriate. There are usually two categories. The more formal short sermon needs to be carefully written, like one of Alistair Cooke's *Letters from America*, with scripted informality. The less formal short sermon requires equally careful preparation, but the preacher takes with him no more than a small prompt on which are written a few cues to remind him of the progress he intends to make. In this case he must rely on a close rapport with his congregation, in part responding to their reactions. In both cases, brevity does not mean ill-preparedness or shoddy delivery.

One of my pet hates is the preacher who, as soon as he steps into the pulpit, removes his wrist-watch with an enormous flourish and places it on the book stand, usually with half its strap dangling over the front. The family of one such preacher described this important ceremony as 'Dad's most meaningless gesture'!

NOTES

[1] The quotation from Thomas Betterton is variously rendered and attributed to a number of people: this is quoted from Donald Coggan, *The Ministry of the Word* (Lutterworth: London, 1964), p 106.

[2] Gerhard Ebeling, *The Nature of Faith* (Collins: London, 1961), p 15.

[3] W S Swaine, *Parson's Pleasure* (1934), p 79, quoted from J R W Stott, *I Believe in Preaching* (Hodder and Stoughton: London, 1982), p 142.

[4] Albert Dawson, *Joseph Parker* (Partridge: London, 1901), p 140.

[5] A W Brown, *Recollections of the Conversation Parties of the Rev. Charles Simeon* (1863), p 189.

[6] J R W Stott, *op cit*, p 292.

[7] *ibid*, p 294.

[8] P T Forsyth, *Positive Preaching and the Modern Mind*

(Independent: London, 3rd ed, 1949), p 75.

[9] H H Farmer, *The Servant of the Word* (Nisbet: London, 1941), p 75.

[10] A G Ferrers Howell, *S. Bernardino of Siena* (1913), p 219.

[11] Thomas Birch, *The Life of the Most Reverend Dr. John Tillotson* (1752), p 19.

[12] W Fraser Mitchell, *English Pulpit Oratory from Andrewes to Tillotson* (1932), p 78.

[13] *The Charges of Samuel Horsley, LLD, FRS, FAS,* (1830), p 4.

[14] Donald Coggan, *On Preaching* (SPCK: London, 1978), p 48.

Chapter 4

WHAT, NO PULPIT!:
George and the Dragon

George went storming out of the church vowing never to go near the place again! One of the stewards chased after him to see if he could help, but that ended in a stand-up row because it turned out that the steward's wife was in the church dance group. Yes, that was the trouble: the dance group! It was simply the last straw for George. This modernising of the Gospel, he thought, had gone too far. He was going home to write a letter straight to the bishop protesting about the lascivious display of female flesh in the house of prayer, the outright denial of all that's pure and holy in the Bible, a desecration of Christian worship: carnal, lustful, idolatrous triviality with clapping and smiling and, worst of all, people waving their arms in the air! If the bishop wouldn't stop this, then George was ready to head a campaign to see right prevail. This must be, he thought, the dragon seen in the vision of John (Revelation 12), and George Verity was ready for the fight. George's views may have been extreme, but they are not offensive in themselves; what is offensive is his conviction that, since he must be right, everyone else must be wrong!

By the time he'd calmed down a bit, George began to worry about one thing which he couldn't explain to himself: why so few others seemed bothered. Normally, when he was heading a campaign to defend the truth, his first allies were those who believed in an unchanging Church in a changing world. But on this occasion they didn't seem to be very worked up. What George hadn't realised was that the church dance group had been formed some time before (without his knowledge), and just after Christmas when

George was away for a few days, they'd illustrated a hymn in church with a dance. Needless to say, there was a reaction at the time, but even that had been muted because everyone could see how well prepared the dancers were, and it was Christmas, so the dust soon settled. When the Sunday School came dancing into church on Palm Sunday waving the paper palms they had just made and singing *All Glory, Laud and Honour*, people were already more relaxed. So by now the dance group did not seem so unnatural to most of the congregation. I'm afraid it's going to take longer to convince George: what he wants is hymns, readings, some prayers and what Samuel Pepys called 'a good, honest and painful sermon' (*Diary* for 1661).[1] Without a proper sermon delivered from the pulpit, there's no worship! On the other hand, most of us are less conscious (and self-conscious) of movement in church than previous generations of Christians have often been—even those who habitually moved around the building to receive Holy Communion and knelt, sat and stood in worship.

Does all preaching have to be pulpit preaching? Some Christians will give a clear answer—a definite YES. Others may be happy to agree in general, without excluding other forms of communication of the word of God. A third group is not bothered whether there's a sermon or not! Donald Coggan recounts an argument he had with a church architect after the dedication of a reordered church, the pulpit of which had been replaced with 'a poor, paltry little stand':

> 'When will you ecclesiastical architects,' I said, 'give us *Anglican* ecclesiastical architecture? Is it not time that a visitor from some other tradition than ours should be able to see, by the very architecture of the building, that Anglicanism is "bifocal" in its means of grace, that the living God comes to us *both* in the sacrament of the Body and Blood of Christ *and* in the sacrament of the Word?'[2]

The point he was making is by no means restricted to Anglican architecture; it could as easily apply to any other Christian tradition. The pulpit is half of that important balance of the sacrament of bread and wine and the sacrament of the word.

ALTERNATIVES

So when I argue for alternatives and supplements to the pulpit, I am in no way seeking to distort the bifocal nature of Christian worship. What I want to say is that the pulpit is not invariably the best means of communication for the Christian gospel within the fellowship of the Church; there are other possibilities which, though they need a great deal of preparation and restraint in their use (otherwise they will become tiresome), ought to be explored. It seems to me that the biblical understanding of proclaiming the word of the Lord has nothing to do with furniture or specific technique. Francis de Sales (1567–1622) wrote: 'The test of a preacher is that his congregation goes away saying, not "What a lovely sermon!" but "I will do something!"'[3] It is not important *how* the word of the Lord comes to people, but that it should *come*.

The Value of Symbols

Let's take a look at the use of symbols in the Bible: sensory images which support, and in some cases are more powerful than spoken proclamation. There is a silly exaggeration of Christian truth, to which I think Mr Verity may be prone, that condemns all forms of symbolism out of hand —at least *religious* symbolism, because of course all of us are familiar with symbols of every kind in our daily lives.

In the Old Testament, symbolic images abound. The scapegoat (Leviticus 16:20–22) driven out into the wild was a symbol of divine forgiveness by the transfer of human guilt to another. When the people of Israel wandering through the wilderness were bitten by snakes, God told Moses to make a bronze snake which was held up on a pole for the healing of all who looked at it (Numbers 21:4–9 and John 3:14–15). The prophet Samuel tore his cloak to demonstrate the tearing of the kingdom from King Saul because of his sins (I Samuel 15:26–29). Isaiah went around naked for three years as a sign that the kingdom of Assyria would denude Egypt and Sudan (Isaiah 20). Jeremiah hid his nice new linen shorts in rocks by the River Euphrates and ruined them to depict how the pride of Judah and Jerusalem would be spoiled (Jeremiah 13:1–11); he bought and smashed a clay jar to symbolise the irreparable fragmentation of God's people and of his city (Jeremiah 19:10–12); he wore an ox yoke to tell the people of God's supremacy and to alert them to Hananiah's false optimism (Jeremiah 27:1–2, 10–17); he bought a field at Anathoth as a sign of the future hope God had in store for the land (Jeremiah 32:6–15).

Again, Ezekiel made a makeshift model of the siege of Jerusalem and acted out three other prophecies of the desolation of the city (Ezekiel 4 and 5). The tale of Jonah is quite possibly a powerful analogy of obedience to God and the greatness of his mercy. Hosea is instructed to act out a life of symbolism by marrying a woman who would be unfaithful, to depict the faithlessness of the people (Hosea 1:2). In the New Testament, the parables of Jesus are strong word-pictures: stories with clear visual images of eternal truths rather than pulpit-sermons. Anyone who is in the least familiar with the Gospels will remember the parables of the good Samaritan, the lost coin, the lost sheep and the lost son, the mustard seed, the Pharisee and the tax collector, the rich fool, the rich man and Lazarus, the shrewd manager, the sower, the ten girls at the wedding, and so on.

These are *active, concrete* symbols, sometimes illustrating a deeper truth, sometimes clothing eternity in flesh. Yet there is a deeper level of symbolism behind much Hebrew and Christian teaching, for the Bible often unites the symbols it uses with the realities behind the symbols. Historical events and the signs and memorials of those events are closely interwoven. For instance, throughout the Bible the term 'Passover' can carry several meanings: the event told in Exodus chapter 12, or the sacrificial Passover animal (I Corinthians 5:7), or the annual celebration of the Passover festival (Mark 14:12). The passage of the people of Israel through the sea is related both as an historical fact and a symbolic reality, evocative of God's power to save his people; so is the experience of the wilderness wanderings; so is the exile in Babylon—the examples are many. In our adoration of the spoken and the written word we have lost sight of the simple fact that all words in all languages are themselves only symbols to describe real things—the only reality in the words themselves, apart from what they mean, is as shapes on paper or sound vibrations in the air.

Christians should be more aware than any others of the unity of symbol and reality, for Jesus Christ, the Word of God, the power of creation, the Word of the Lord on the lips of the prophets, is revealed not as a holy guru who points us to truth, nor as a symbol—shapes on a page or sounds in the air—but as Reality himself. The message of the New Testament is not only that this 'Word' is real but also that he is flesh: 'The Word became a human being and, full of grace and truth, lived among us. We saw his glory, the glory which he received as the Father's only Son' (John 1:14). Notice John saying that we *saw* the glory of the *word*. In his first letter, John writes about 'the Word of life' and says that we 'have *heard* it and we have *seen* it with our eyes; yes, we have *seen* it, and our hands have *touched* it.' (1 John 1:1). Here is a description of God's Word who is not simply speech or writing but the living, breathing God-in-man; for the coming of Christ as a child at Bethlehem is the becoming human of God, the eternal Word taking on other dimensions. Thus, when Jesus proclaims his 'I am...' sayings recorded in Saint John's Gospel—'I am the bread of life (John 6:35), ... the light of the world (John 8:12), ... the gate

(John 10:9), ... the good shepherd (John 10:11), ... the resurrection and the life (John 11:25), ... the way, the truth, and the life (John 14:6), ... the vine' (John 15:1 and 5), and in the Revelation, 'the first and the last and the living one, the beginning and the end' (Revelation 21:6)—he is saying something beyond the power of words alone to express, and is consecrating far more than simply the spoken or the written word as a means for communicating himself. No wonder the listeners reacted so violently to Jesus' putting flesh onto spiritual imagery!

There is a very powerful symbol with which Christians are familiar: the Lord's Supper, often described as an *effectual sign*. Whatever your own particular view of this sacrament may be, those words 'this is my body' and 'this is my blood of the new covenant' must express more than a visual aid to faith; more than a simple reminder of Jesus, given the closeness of symbol to reality in biblical thinking. This is part of Christian experience. Recently, one of my parishioners, nearly a century old, fell and fractured his femur while preparing to come to Communion in church, and I found myself taking him Communion at home while he waited for the ambulance to take him to hospital. After our short service, he thanked me: 'I feel stronger *inside* now.' The Word of God comes to us in more than words, and there are times when mere words are not enough to express him.

George Verity says he has no time for symbolism, but he cannot avoid it, of course, unless he insists on ignoring all traffic signs when he drives his car! And it happens under his nose in church, as well. In his tradition, they stand to hear the Gospel at the eucharist, physically reminding them that Christ is central to the Scriptures and that the Bible is, like the Passover meal, food for action. He may notice many people turning towards the reader, a sign that they mean to pay attention to the word rather than gazing at their feet in apparent disinterest. When it comes to praying, he does his best to avoid kneeling which, for some unknown reason, he regards as a bit suspect, but he dutifully bows his head and looks religious in just as significant a way. When it comes to Communion, he notices certain important gestures—the taking of bread and wine, a meaningful breaking of the bread—and then he gets out of his seat and moves forward in an unconscious acting out of his faith in Christ as he comes to receive the elements. He hasn't even noticed the symbolic meaning of the furniture:

> God is here; as we his people
> meet to offer praise and prayer...
> Here are symbols to remind us
> of our lifelong need of grace;
> here are table, font and pulpit,
> here the cross has central place;
> here in honesty of preaching,
> here in silence as in speech,
> here in newness and renewal
> God the Spirit comes to each.

(F Pratt Green[4])

So let us have a look at some alternatives and supplements to the pulpit. Let us see how other media can enable the Church to shout: *Listen to the word of the Lord!*

Music

This is, as we all know, one of the most powerful of art forms, and it can be used easily in conjuction with prayer, with Bible reading and with preaching. There is hardly anything in God's creation which can fill me with more inner rapture than some of the music of Monteverdi, or J S Bach, or Elgar—what little I know of the art of music falls far short of explaining its power in my mind and heart. Music can help to create an atmosphere or to set a scene as well as—or even better than—many words; it can be used to conclude an act of worship by providing the right atmosphere in which people can respond to God's call; and it can be used as an interlude between parts of worship, when the mind needs a moment to catch up and to meditate. A single work can sometimes replace a whole service: not only such things as J S Bach's *Christmas Oratorio* (several services!), or his *Saint Matthew* and *Saint John Passions*, or his *B Minor Mass*, or even Handel's *Messiah* (all of which are far beyond the musical abilities of most churches), but also one of the many lowlier pop cantatas (such as *Captain Noah and His Floating Zoo*) can be in themselves almost complete acts of teaching, praying, worshipping and preaching.

We see in many churches that after the century or so in which the organ has reigned musically supreme, it is beginning to give way to a more traditional variety of instrumental accompaniment, and the kind of choirs that imagined they were rivals to the great and the famous (but unfortunately were not!) are generally giving way to smaller groups. In a time of such change, it is appropriate that the new patterns which develop should belong to the whole structure of worship, to the preaching as well as to the praying and the teaching. A great deal depends on the breadth of taste in your church organist or director of music: if he's hooked on 'Sankey' or considers anything not published by the Royal School of Church Music beneath his notice, you're in trouble!

Reading

While strongly discouraging the straight reading of sermons, there is undoubtedly a place for straightforward reading within worship and specifically, within the context of teaching and preaching. There is, in the first place, the extended biblical reading, such as reading the entire letter of Paul to the Philippians in a dynamic translation. I remember an occasion in my own church in which we were struggling with the many difficulties of interpreting chapters 9–11 of the Letter to the Romans, and I was not sure that we had come to an altogether satisfactory conclusion—which, if you know the passage, will not surprise you! So, with a group of young people, mainly students and folk in their first jobs, we read those three chapters in the translation by J B Phillips. The effect was astonishing (to me, at least): all of a sudden, with the whole canvas of the argument before us, the picture began to emerge.

There may also be occasions for retelling biblical stories in your own words, perhaps with some characterisation. Or you could write up your own extended parable based on a biblical verse; for instance, Isaiah 9:2 has enormous potential for a Christmas tale:

> The people who walked in darkness
> have seen a great light.
> They lived in a land of shadows,
> but now light is shining on them.

It is, incidentally, one of the most important aspects of preaching to be able to 'tell the tale' in your own words. (See p 143.)

In the second place, there may be readings from some later part of the Christian story: extracts or summaries of part of the life of a great Christian, or small cameos from the lives of God's ordinary saints. I think of the beautiful story of Arope, an eight-year-old Ethiopian boy who, in order to maintain contact with the local Christian mission, carried the teacher's Bible along a difficult and dangerous path between the mission house and the school every day for two years. One day, he was missing, and it turned out that he had been killed defending another boy from a crocodile. When Arope's mother met the mission teacher, she told him of the beatings she had given her boy to stop him fulfilling this obligation: 'I'd like to know who this person is who could make a boy do that.' In the village of the illiterate Arope there is now a Christian community. That is just a summary of one such moving story.

In the third place, there is poetry: a vast array of contemporary Christian poetry very easily available, and the best of the Christian poetry of the past. Some of it has found its way into our hymns, but there is a good deal more waiting to be discovered and used in worship and for preaching.

In the fourth place, there are specially-written stories. Only a generation or two earlier than ours, there was a good deal of scepticism about whether telling stories was appropriate in the context of worship because, it was thought, they lacked dignity. No doubt you, like me, have heard Christians of the present day rejecting allegories which use animal characters because they think that the Christian story will be equated with childish fables, and we hear of those who expend their energy on writing letters to Christian newspapers objecting to Santa Claus! You must make up your own mind, but I believe we seriously misjudge human nature if we do not recognise the importance of fables in teaching truth—Aesop knew that in the sixth century before Christ; allegorical stories can clothe truth in flesh (even if it is animal flesh). John Bunyan's *Pilgrim's Progress* and the series of Narnia books by C S Lewis are typical of this type of writing, except on a grander scale, but carefully selected extracts could well be read in worship and might make more sense than some of our sermons! If you try your hand at story-writing, you may well discover you have a gift for it. There were, of course, George Veritys in the seventeenth century when Bunyan wrote *Pilgrim's Progress*, and in his Apology for the book, he defends his use of allegory. First, he has the precedent of greater saints; second, he notes that great men have written 'Dialogue-wise', for God 'makes base things usher in divine'; and third,

I find that Holy Writ in many places
Hath semblance with this method, where the cases
Doth call for one thing to set forth another.

Several years ago, as part of the practice of entrusting the monthly 'Family Worship' to groups of Christians, one group decided to abandon the usual talk and one of their number wrote a story. In summary, it was about three sons who inherited from their father what appeared to be an empty wooden box: a box which, for those with faith, became defender and provider; a box which was destroyed in anger by fire, only to be resurrected as three small boxes, one for each brother. One of them ignored his box and came to a sticky end, another admired his box on the mantelpiece and dusted it religiously, and the third used this gift from his father. The parallels with Christ's gift of the Spirit and the mission of the Church are obvious (see John 20:21–22).

In the fifth place, readings of extracts from books of popular theology might be considered for the right occasion. Over the course of a year or two, I read Emil Brunner's magnificent little book *Our Faith*⁵ to a fairly small congregation at an early morning service, and then I based my evening sermon in another church on the same theme, often using the same superb illustrations. I hope those who heard the readings and the sermons gained from them; the preacher certainly did. Brunner's book did not require much editing, apart from a little updating here and there, but other books may require a few adaptations and probably some subdivision.

There is a warning to issue here: a gift for reading aloud is not as common as many people suppose. There are many people who read the Bible in our churches today whose gifts must lie elsewhere, and there are others—including clergy— who ruin readings by dullness or by deathbed enthusiasm or by being strangely unable to avoid stressing every preposition they come across! Few enthusiastic, bad readers will ever seek the help they certainly need.

Reading and Music can be very effectively combined in the proper balance, but they can also be cheap and nasty. Unless you have one of those brilliant musicians who can extemporise and read your mind at the same time, both the reading and the music need to be well prepared. I quoted earlier in the chapter a verse from the introduction to the fourth Gospel (John 1:1–18). That passage has a pattern to it, the thought at the beginning matching the thought at the end, the second thought matching the penultimate thought, and so on until we reach the thought which stands alone at the apex, the climax, the heart of the passage, verse 12 as we should call it: 'Some, however, did receive him and believed in him; so he gave them the right to become God's children.' A skilful musician can at least suggest something of this pattern in accompanying the spoken word.

Interviews

There are various ways of using interviews, as the introduction to a time of intercession, as an effective way of passing on important information, or as a substitute for a monologue sermon. Take, for instance, the plight of some poor, returned mission partner from overseas: she is a nurse (or a teacher or an engineer or an administrator or whatever) and has never been called upon to speak in public before a sophisticated audience—why should she, for God did not provide her with those gifts? But in the deputation work of her home leave she finds herself asked to preach nine sermons! Panic immediately sets in. There is, however, one wise minister among the churches to which she is going, who recognises her fears and difficulties and offers instead to conduct an interview in which she can say just as much as she would have said in a sermon, with far more freedom, far less fear and probably far more effect. Of course, the two parties to an interview need to know where they are going and it is important to have a run-through beforehand. It is most effective when the interviewer has no more than a few simple questions on a small card and the interviewee has none; this can only be achieved when the two have each others' confidence. Interviews can help to relate one individual's personal witness to the problems of another who is listening, and they can create interest in subjects that might be thought dull. It is sometimes interesting to stage an interview with some biblical or historical character, such as the apostle Peter on the night of the first Easter Day, looking back on those last few critical days, or Naomi reflecting on an eventful life. A good deal of preparation will be needed, because, for this to be effective, the person playing the part of Peter or Naomi must be very familiar with the character and with the events of his or her life in order to avoid anything but the lightest scripting.

Dialogue

This is an extension of the interview, though more formal, and it is possibly the most important form of teaching in the history of education. In its straightforward question-and-answer form it is a basic element in New Testament teaching. The background can be traced from the pagan Socrates (470–399 BC), whose followers developed it into a kind of intellectual game, and Plato (428–347 BC), whose contribution was to develop the technique into a drama of ideas. It is found in the Wisdom literature of the Old Testament, particularly in the book of Job. Jesus was very familiar with the dialogue technique of teaching and it occurs frequently in the Gospels:

> Tell me, who do people say I am?...
> Who do you say I am?...
> Tell me, where did John's right to baptise come from: was it from God or from man?...
> Whose face and name are these?
> (Mark 8:27 and 29; 11:30; 12:16)

The New Testament letters contain strong echoes of the Stoic diatribes, in which imaginary objectors are answered by the teacher: and so the apostle Paul appears to conduct a conversation with himself on occasions, notably in Romans 3:1–8 and 27–31. Paul was not alone: there has been a powerful Christian tradition of dialogue-teaching since then, including such famous exponents as Augustine, Gregory, Anselm, Aquinas, Wyclif, Baxter, Berkeley, Swift, and innumerable others. Although it was Martin Luther, between 1517 and 1525, who invented what we know today as the catechism, a formal doctrinal play with two actors, it was no more than a natural convergence of two existing methods: teaching by question-and-answer and the formal dialogue. So this is no new-fangled method of communication in the Church!

Until relatively recently in many churches, particularly Anglican and Lutheran, Sunday afternoons were given over in part to catechising. At its best, that did not mean parrot-fashion theology for children but the use of the catechism to provide a helpful introduction for a more informal sermon. In the late 1970's, the American Episcopal Church Catechism or *Outline of the Faith* was written with liturgical use in mind. Yet, apart from plain catechisms (which would need a little doctoring because most of them are notoriously out of date), there are other possibilities for the use of dialogue in preaching. A formal dialogue could be used in much the same way as the interview I have already suggested with some biblical character or Christian whose teaching has significantly affected the Church's life. Thus, a series of questions might be devised on Saint Paul's teaching about 'the Christian and God's Law', the answers coming directly from Paul's own writings. Clearly, the translation would need to be dynamic, and both the questions and the readings very carefully selected. The technique could, however, be helpful in presenting difficult, abstract themes. Another option might be a dialogue from some Christian novel or allegory—the kind of thing we're all familiar with from *The Pilgrim's Progress*, or even *The Lord of the Rings*. Alternatively, you could adapt some of the published 'questions' about the Christian faith, such as Colin Chapman's *Christianity on Trial*[6]: this particular series of books, written almost as a dialogue, would be easy to work with. Or you might set up some topical questions and use extracts from the Bible or reflections on the Bible to answer them. There is a lot of life left in the dialogue!

Special monologues

There are many published monologues, most of them with a semi-humorous approach, dealing with biblical events and subjects. The masters of this genre are Bob Newhart, Garrison Keillor, and the late Joyce Grenfell—those who knew Joyce Grenfell's schoolroom monologues could almost describe her little Sidney, the sort of awkward child you end up sitting next to on a bus! There are many religious plays and anthologies with some superb monologues: Becket's sermon in the Interlude of *Murder in the Cathedral* by T S Eliot, and his *Journey of the Magi* or *A Song for Simeon*, and several soliloquies from John Arden's *The Business of Good Government*, to name just a few; writers of secular literature can also be a valuable source of material for reading-preaching.

Drama

This covers a wide range, from pieces which are genuinely dramatic to light sketches illustrating a single point. There should be no difficulty in finding material, though it is more difficult to fit the piece to the occasion. If you are gifted or know someone who is, you could even write your own.

Drama is an old Christian tradition. Modern revivals of the mediaeval mystery and passion plays are often as powerful as their modern counterparts. Even the annual Sunday School Nativity play falls into this category, though I could lead you to not a few parents whose faces pale at the very mention of Nativity plays. I know of one church where the same play had been used for so long that the parents of children who were now learning its unutterable doggerel could remember with pain the same speeches from their own childhood! It would be wise for the powers that be in any church to set a rule for the regular changing of the Nativity play—there is no shortage of good material. In the case of children acting, enthusiasm and simplicity of heart are all that anyone can desire, but that is not the case where adults are concerned. For adult drama, simple enthusiasm is not sufficient. There must be some signs of a gift from God and of the actors' intention to consecrate that gift with some serious study of the art. Wooden and self-conscious acting in church, as much as angry axe-grinding, is worse than disastrous because the glory of God is at stake.[7]

Mime

Mime is a link between drama and dance. It may be narrated by the spoken word, accompanied by music or performed in silence. It can be used to tell a story or even, with care, to preach a theme; with some rehearsal, to make sure that the actors are in the right place at the right time, it can be a very effective means of illustrating a sermon. For instance, a sermon on a tough subject like 'justification' could be illustrated half-way through (at the right moment logically and before the congregation drifts into a theologically-induced stupor) with a mime of the heavy weight of the demands of God's Law crushing Everyman until the Son of God appears and places himself underneath the weight, lifting the load from the sinner's back. Having died under the Law, the Son stands hand-in-hand with the justified sinner on top of the Law, right with God.

Dance

Dance is a more formalised development of mime and normally accompanied by music. Anyone who is familiar with ballet (which I am not) will know that it can be used very effectively to tell a complete story, but within the context of Christian worship, it is used most frequently to illustrate singing or to depict some biblical account or emotion. Since it normally takes a great deal of preparation and practice, it would be rare to find dance replacing preaching, but it can be a most helpful supplement. For instance, a sermon on the second coming of Christ could well be expressed in a group dancing the hymn, *The King of Glory Comes, the Nation Rejoices*!

A word of warning: the art of dance does require professional advice at some level. A great deal of what is called
'Spirit-inspired' dance is highly applauded by the dancers
themselves, their relations and admirers, but looks to the
rest of us like arm-flinging and meaningless twirling! Dance
is an art form in which there are specialised techniques (and
exercises to go with them!) as there are for drama, music
and the visual arts. You may find help from Rosemary
Budd's book *Moving Prayer*.[8]

Activity-preaching

Many preachers have problems with all-age worship. It is
very difficult to avoid the trap of speaking at one of two
levels—to the children or to the adults—or else to be jug-
gling between the two, and, considering the likely age-range
of the children, the only people who might get anything out
of it are a few adults! Anyone who has tried it knows exactly
what I mean. Charles Simeon's image of a preacher trying to
fill some narrow-necked bottles with a large pail of water
comes to mind. The difficulties are increased by the talk having normally to be delivered with few notes and to be, at
least in part, responsive to the reactions of the congregation.

I have found that dividing what I have to say into two
parts, a factual unit and a practical unit, is a helpful way of
overcoming the problem. The first unit, the factual, can use
any kind of activity in order to teach the basic facts which
the preacher is trying to convey: this could be a quiz or the
children blowing party-trumpets around the imaginary
walls of Jericho, or something illustrated on an overhead
projector, or it may involve a discovery—the options are
enormous. This unit is followed by a break, perhaps an
appropriate song, and then the practical, short talk which
aims to strike the point swiftly and exactly.

On other occasions, when children may be in for part of
the principal Sunday service—and we have no right to
refuse a proper place to children in the worship of the
church at least once a Sunday—someone should be given

the job of speaking to the children and of introducing something special for them. In our church, we have a rota of the various group leaders who run the children's sessions, and often these leaders have most ingenious ways of illustrating the unifying theme of the children's groups. All sorts of exciting things can come out of a plastic shopping bag!

The best of these little talks are the short ones, well illustrated with practical things that all the children can understand, and the funniest ones are those which evoke some unlikely response. We all looked a bit puzzled on Trinity Sunday when one mum asked us to think of words beginning with 'tri-'. We got as far as 'tricycle' and 'triangle' when one little boy shouted out 'TRICERATOPS.' There's not a lot you can say after that!

Several years ago I had the privilege of hearing a sister in one of the religious orders preaching at a Good Friday service. We were each to bring a hammer with us, and the nails, the small pieces of wood and rope were provided. During the course of that service, each of us made a small cross and we were powerfully reminded of our own part in crucifying the Lord of glory. What's more, as I travelled around in pastoral contacts for some time after, I kept coming across those powerful symbols of that meaningful occasion. There are many other tactile symbols which can be used to enhance preaching.

Video

The scope for using pre-recorded video tapes in preaching and teaching is growing daily and, as the technology becomes cheaper and more sophisticated, it is bound to have as important an impact on the church's life as it has already had on our society. It is an area where copyright issues may be particularly critical. A good interview with a Christian of some significance, and the right treatment of special subjects (such as a series I saw recently on the history and use of the Psalms, or an important study of the Christian approach to a contemporary moral issue), and historical sketches of the lives of Christians, recorded from television programmes, may be profitable. Most agencies of Christian mission have now caught up with the video revolution; it is significant that those who were responsible for beginning the preparations for the 1988 Lambeth Conference of Anglican bishops used video very effectively to communicate their message to the whole Anglican Communion worldwide.

Discussions

There is no reason why a preacher must continue to spout on his own for an extended period of time every time he enters the pulpit. Perhaps it would be better to prepare a small sermon and to hand out pieces of paper with prepared questions for discussion, having first carefully scattered group leaders among the congregation. Or it may be better to give three or four brief introductions and, between each one, to get people talking in buzz-groups (groups of people within gossiping-distance of one another). These occasions need to be well prepared, and those responsible for helping the groups with their task need to get into action swiftly. There is little that will provoke the average peace-loving Christian into an imitation of a ravenous lion more than asking him to respond in the presence of other people (unwarned) to what he has heard. This reaction will be extremely fierce if the planning is done badly!

If there are questions, they need to be proper discussion questions, not the kind you could answer with a 'yes/no/don't know'. If there is to be simply an open discussion, everyone needs to know clearly what ought to be happening. The dreaded monopoliser of all Christian discussions needs to be identified and relieved of his monopoly with whatever courage can be mustered! There seems no need for any reporting-back, always a tedious exercise at the best of times. It is probably a good idea not to warn the congregation that a discussion is coming up, or they will immediately find some relation who could come to lunch or tea, preventing them from coming to church; but the leader needs to be gentle. An extension of these in-worship discussions is a question time for the keen ones after the service and perhaps even a day conference before or after a special series of sermons.

Visual images

In many churches nowadays, the sight of a projector screen is not unusual; there will, of course be plenty of people who will object to such a pagan object appearing within the religious building, though I have not as yet discovered what theology lies behind their difficulty. However, I have found that a screen which is a discreet fixture in the building relieves almost all the objections. A large screen is very helpful for an overhead projector, on which the preacher can display maps, family trees, illustrative pictures, subject-headings and so on—Richard Baxter, in the seventeenth century, could have done with one for a 65 point sermon!

Illustrations can be very helpful not only in teaching but also in praying. The final section of a superb filmstrip produced a few years ago by some of the mission agencies, entitled *Mr Global Christian*, was a series of pictures set to the music of Dvořák's *New World Symphony* and reading of verses from Genesis, the Gospels and the Revelation. The mixture of appropriate pictures and some contrasting images combined with the reading of the verses had a powerful effect on the praying of those who looked and listened. We felt reassured that God had made mankind in his own image, then we were shown a picture of a starving woman, moving us deeply in prayer. Visual images, slides, films and filmstrips can also be used to provide information about the Church overseas and background information about the lands of the Bible. And you can easily produce your own slide-sequence to illustrate a parable or a miracle from the ministry of Jesus.

Special events

The major Christian festivals are ideal opportunities for special events involving worship, teaching, prayer, drama, dance, humour, monologue, music, singing, preaching, mime, visual presentation—a whole variety of media all celebrating our faith and our Lord, all teaching us and all proclaiming the certainty of his love. This is the sort of event that a church can work on for itself, either using published material or writing its own. I recall a wonderful celebration we had during my ministry in the country, bringing together two churches to tell the life story of an ordinary man, Simon, who ended up carrying the cross of Jesus. All sorts of people were involved in many expressions of faith and love during that event, but the one which will stick in my mind the longest is the pure gallantry of an ex-army major turned church treasurer dressed up as the prophet Micah. He had every reason to refuse our request to dress up as an eighth-century BC prophet, let alone utter words of doom to an unsuspecting congregation. It was pure genius! Most of the two congregations were involved, and we all learned a great deal through our participation. The best way of all is to get this kind of celebration going on an inter-church basis, especially at Christmas and Easter, when they can be significant acts of corporate witness.

A Note

Please be warned of the danger of copyright. Essentially, the copyright laws, insofar as they affect Christian publications, are there to enable new works to be published: if we all stole the copyright of other people's efforts, considerably fewer new works would see the light of day. A basic knowledge of the law and a commonsense approach to it should be welcomed in all churches.

Any Objections?

However, there are some arguments against using the kind of forms that I have been encouraging in this chapter. I have heard people say of other Christians: 'How can you have anything to do with them? They use drama in their services!' I find this isolationism hard to understand. Sometimes they won't even associate with the people who will associate with people who get up to these antics!

On the other hand, we may be comforted by the fact that most Christians—whether or not they have hesitations about alternatives to the pulpit—are grateful that the word of the Lord is being heard by whatever means. John Stott, for instance, expresses his own hesitations about debate or dialogue in preaching that 'it seems to me, out of place in the context of public worship',[9] but ministers of small churches may well come to different conclusions. He prefers to rely on 'the silent dialogue which should be developing between the preacher and his hearers'—the words of the preacher which provoke questions in their minds which he then proceeds to answer. But there writes a master of the art, and, in any case, it would be unfair to caricature John Stott as an opponent of other forms of preaching-communication: 'Although nothing can supplant preaching,' he writes, 'it definitely needs to be supplemented with additional teaching and discussion activities afterwards.'[10]

Whether George Verity likes it or not, much of his own communication, as with yours and mine, is not verbal but physical. It is seen, heard, touched, even smelt or tasted. The Word of God is not only legible and audible but visible and tangible, for in Christ God has taken on himself our human flesh, and there should be no part of the Christian's life and communication of that Word which can not bring him glory.

NOTES

1 *The Diary of Samuel Pepys* (Latham and Matthews edition) (G Bell: London, 1970), vol 2, year 1661.
2 Donald Coggan, *On Preaching* (SPCK: London, 1978), p 5.
3 Francis de Sales (Bishop of Geneva), *On the Preacher and Preaching* (1964).
4 From *Partners in Praise* (Stainer and Bell).
5 The reference is to Emil Brunner, *Our Faith*, tr J W Rilling (SCM: London, 1949, now out of print).
6 Colin Chapman, *Christianity on Trial* (Lion: Berkhamstead, 1974).
7 For ideas on drama sketches, see Nigel Forde's book *Theatrecraft* (1986); and for sketches and plays ideal in a Christian context, see *Laughter in Heaven* (ed Murray Watts, 1985), *One Stage Further* (Nigel Forde, 1987), and *Playing With Fire* (ed Paul Burbridge, 1987): all published by MARC Europe. Watts, Forde, and Burbridge are all members of the Riding Lights Theatre Company, based in York.
8 MARC Europe, 1987.
9 J R W Stott, *I Believe in Preaching* (Hodder and Stoughton: London, 1982), p 60.
10 *ibid*, p 76.

Chapter 5

GOING BY THE BOOK:
The Doctor's Appeal

> *Yet more there be who doubt God's ways not just,*
> *And to his own edicts, found contradicting,*
> *They give the reins to wandering thought,*
> *Regardless of his glory's diminution;*
> *'Till by their own perplexities involved*
> *They ravel more, still less resolved,*
> *But never find self-satisfying solution.*[1]

Parson Snuffle was very fond of quoting John Milton and, although he knew that this wasn't a specific reference to the Bible, no doubt it was fair to use these lines in defence of God's revelation of himself under attack from one who saw God chiefly revealed in the events of daily life. Dr Lee Ann appreciated the effort that her vicar put into his sermons, but she couldn't understand his general approach. All the preachers she'd ever heard read out a verse from the Bible at the beginning, like a motto, usually repeating it, presumably for the benefit of people with deaf-aids, and then proceeded to make observations about human life with, perhaps, a word or two linking back to the text. Surely that was the modern way of going about things, rooting one's teaching in real life and facing the real issues, challenging middle-class values? (This is Dr Lee Ann's main enemy, though a keen observer might find it difficult to distinguish between her values and those of the middle-classes.)

Any kind of preaching that goes back to the biblical text and tries to bring it into the present must, she thinks, be seriously misguided: the Bible is there to be read as a remarkable collection of ancient documents, reflecting the way that a special people thought of their God, themselves and their world before Christ, and a striking collection of semi-historical and literary works that bear witness to the way Christians developed a new kind of faith in the light of the great man, Jesus of Nazareth. To imagine that these ancient writings could have more than a historical or inspirational value in teaching Christian belief and practice today seems to the good doctor to be quite extraordinary. When she hears people in church refer to the Bible as 'the word of the Lord' she goes along with it only to keep the peace, but for her it has no meaning at all unless some high thought comes into her mind as she hears it read.

Mr Snuffle doesn't see it that way, but his authoritative rendering of seventeenth-century poetry does nothing to convince Lee Ann. 'Please, Septimus,' she pleads, 'don't keep trying to push the Bible onto us! There's so much of the Bible that has no relevance to us at all, and the rest is at least 1900 years old—it's bound to be vastly out of touch with the problems of real people today. Please, I appeal to you, give us some of your own advice on contemporary issues; hang it on a text if you want, but don't try to force the Bible down our throats!' The parson knows that what she says to him openly as a friend, many others are thinking. They may not be able to put it into words, but, if they want a sermon at all, they want some advice about their problems, and they don't think that the Bible has the answers to those problems. They want something practical, some instructions on how to behave in given circumstances, and they simply can't cope with a book which purports to be 'God's word written' and yet which looks just like an anthology of poetry, history, fable, and fiction.

If there had been any teachers among them, Dr Lee Ann believed, they might have suggested that a book intended to teach should start at the place where its readers begin, and gradually progress through to the point at which the reader is familiar with the subject. So, if the Bible was like a *Teach*

Yourself French book, it would begin with a few things we all know about France and the language: it would tell us about the major differences in construction between our language and French; it would give us manageable quantities to learn and exercises at every stage to consolidate our learning; then we'd soon pick it up. So, we could begin with very little knowledge of the language and, at the end of the book, with some practice, ought to be OK for next summer's holiday on the Continent.

If this was the kind of book the Bible was, Dr Lee Ann and her friends would have no problem with biblical preaching. But it is not, and they have recognised that it's not—it's not simply a textbook for learning the Christian religion; it's not a *Teach Yourself Getting to Know God* and it's not an instruction manual like the thing you find in the glove-box of a new car with full details of how to operate all life's gadgets, and a troubleshooting section to help you sort out all life's problems. The *Bible* is what the name literally means, a library of books, varying in age, background, type, style, content and context. It's quite acceptable to the modern mind to read little bits of this ancient and holy collection of 66 books, but it is quite another thing to try and preach it for what it claims to be: the Word of the Lord for today!

Dr Lee Ann left the parson a confused and perplexed man. Was it, maybe, his less than fluent manner in the pulpit and his occasional over-long sermons which had caused this disaffection with the Bible? Or is it true that biblical preaching is no more than striving after the ideals of the past, and that what is needed for today is contemporary thinking on current issues?

Parson Snuffle's worries are shared by many preachers today—we should not underestimate the problem—but these worries are not merely the products of our own age. Eighteenth-century rationalism said that the *facts* (that is, the miracles, etc) contained in the Gospels could be interpreted by nature and human reason without recourse to theories of the supernatural: there were, they assumed, logical explanations for all the supernatural 'facts'. And later, men like David Friedrich Strauss, in the early years of the nineteenth century, rejected even the 'facts' as needing any historical base: 'The supernatural birth of Christ, his miracles, his resurrection and ascension, remain eternal truths, whatever doubt may be cast on their reality as historical facts.'[2] Parson Snuffle's heart told him otherwise, nor was his mind convinced. The Bible still has remarkable power in the Christian's life—he knows that. In 1967, J B Phillips wrote one of the most significant Christian paperbacks, *Ring of Truth*, to defend the New Testament against the charge that it is an unreliable guide. He wrote for 'the ordinary man who is no theologian', and he was angry at those who undermined the Scriptures.

> A clergyman, old, retired, useless if you like, took his own life because of his reading of the 'New Theology' and even some programmes on television finally drove him, in his loneliness and ill-health, to conclude that his own life's work had been founded on a lie. He felt that these highly qualified writers and speakers must know so much more than he did, so they must be right... I am *not* concerned to distort or dilute the Christian faith so that modern undergraduates, for example, can accept it without a murmur. I am concerned with the truth revealed in and through Jesus Christ... I therefore felt that it was high time that someone, who has spent the best years of his life in studying the New Testament and good, modern, communicative English, spoke out. I do not care a rap what the *avant garde* scholars say; I do very much care what God says and does.[3]

Without wishing to deny that we have a lot to learn as Christians from the theology of today, let it be heard clearly that the theology of the Bible—and, in particular, preaching from the Bible—is not a thing of the past. The pressures on the preacher—from professional theologians on the one side and self-styled down-to-earth Christians on the other— can be very hard to resist. But resisted they must be.

THE BASIS

The Bible has been the basis for Christian preaching since the beginning of the Christian Church, a perfectly natural development from the scripturally-based practices of the Hebrews, 'the People of the Book' as they have been called. Donald Coggan notes that it could never have been said of the apostolic preachers, as it could be said of some modern ones, that their text was: 'God so loved the world that He inspired a certain Jew to teach that there was a good deal to be said for loving one another',[4] for all the evidence we have of preaching in the early centuries of the Christian era is that it was profoundly biblical.

The Acts of the Apostles, for instance, is full of examples of biblical preaching (some of which we'll come back to later); the nearest equivalent to a church sermon is Paul preaching in the synagogue at Pisidian Antioch, recorded in chapter 13, verses 16–43. Here Luke provides us with a summary of a three-phase expository sermon: first, the story of Israel is explained as the story of God's salvation, culminating in the coming of the Son of David, the Saviour of Israel (verses 16–25); second, Jesus is the Saviour, put to death in man's blindness to the truth and raised in fulfilment of the Scriptures (verses 26–37); third, the message of freedom from sin by faith in Christ is the reason for Paul's preaching (verses 38–43). Although there is no possibility of Paul citing any of the Gospels at this stage in his ministry (or at any point in his ministry, for the Gospels arrived later), he not only uses the Scriptures of the Old Testament but also proclaims the work of God in the person of Christ (the heart of the New Testament Scriptures). The lengthy process of establishing what books should form the New Testament, a process which went on for the best part of 300 years after Paul, established these books as having the same divine authority over God's people as the Old Testament Scriptures. What we see recorded in Acts 13 is not only evidence of preaching from the Old Testament but also of preaching the central (though unwritten) facts of the New. Justin Martyr, for instance, writing his *First Apology* about a century after the Apostle, provides us with clear evidence of the importance of the Scriptures in Christian preaching at that early stage in the life of the Church. This is reflected in the sermons and reports of sermons of many leading Christian figures in the ensuing centuries. From the very first, Christian preaching has been biblical.

Yet it is not simply because the Bible has always had an important place in the past that we can argue for its importance in the present. There is a far more human reason: the Bible commands our attention in a way we cannot fully explain. Though its variety is enormous and meets us at many points of need, it speaks to us with an extraordinary divine command, that same uncanny authority noticed by people who listened to the young preacher from Nazareth. Augustine (354–430) had a long struggle with God in his dissolute youth and could not allow himself to become so childlike as to allow the Scriptures to have power over his life, though he could not resist them! One day in AD 386, he reopened the letter of Paul to the Romans:

> I seized, opened, and in silence read the passage upon which my eyes first fell... 'no orgies or drunkenness, no immorality or indecency, no fighting or jealousy. But take up the weapons of the Lord Jesus Christ, and stop paying attention to your sinful nature and satisfying its desires' [Romans 13:13b and 14]. No further would I read; nor was there need; for instantly at the end of this sentence, as though my heart were flooded with a light of peace, all the shadows of doubt melted away.[5]

Martin Luther (1483–1546) described his conversion, which came through the study of the Scriptures in perplexity at the state of the Church and of his own soul: 'Then I felt that I was born again and entered through open doors into paradise.'[6] John Bunyan (1628–1688) had a similarly harrowing experience of conversion, again through the power of the Bible: 'Conversion is not the smooth, easy-going process some seem to think it, otherwise man's heart would never have been compared to fallow ground, and God's Word to the plough.'[7] John Wesley (1703–1791) was converted as he listened to the reading of Luther's commentary on Romans, especially chapter 1, verse 17, an occasion he described more fully in his *Journal* as exchanging 'the faith of a servant' for 'the faith of a son... Then it pleased God to kindle a fire which I trust shall never be extinguished.'[8]

Again in one of the general instructions of the Roman Catholic *Missal*, the importance of the Bible and of biblical preaching is underlined:

> ... when the Scriptures are read in the Church, God himself speaks to his people and it is Christ, present in his word, who proclaims the Gospel... a homily as a living expression of the word, increases its effectiveness and is an integral part of the service.[9]

The important place given to Bible-reading and biblical preaching in Christian worship is attested by the whole history of the Church and by the Bible's mysterious ability to meet human need. Further, can you think of a significant renewal of Christian faith in the history of the Church which has not been inspired by and nurtured on a renewal of Bible study? In his excellent book, *The Authority of the Old Testament*, John Bright makes a plea—

> for a return to biblical preaching generally, which is to say, to preaching based in the authority of the biblical Word... The strength of the church lies in the gospel it proclaims—thus in its preaching—today, as it always has. And since the church stands under the authority of

the Word, it follows that the best preaching—nay, the only proper preaching—is biblical preaching. Only biblical preaching carries with it the authority of the Word. If, therefore, the Christian pulpit is ever to regain the power and respect which rightfully belongs to it, it will be through a return to biblical preaching.[10]

Parson Snuffle explains to his people that the Bible is like a love-letter from God to the Church: the letter tells us about the extraordinary love God has for us, and, when we fall in love with Jesus, we fall in love with the Word who reveals God. We do not frame the letter and hang it on a wall to be admired, but we treasure it, we keep it close to us, and its pages become soiled as we turn to it in the middle of our chores; we can remember some of its phrases and its truth strengthens us. That kind of love-letter respect for the Bible needs to be revived today, not a silly nit-picking about the spelling mistakes and the crossings-out, nor, on the other hand, an adoration and veneration of its pages as though it were a sacred relic! When we say that the Bible needs to be restored to its central place in the Church and its worship, it is not out of any desire to vaunt the book, but that this book has a God-given ability to draw us to him.

THE GAP

One of the problems faced by any Christian communicator of the Bible is the gap that exists between where we are and where the Bible was written, in time, in place and in culture. We have not only to take the Bible and put it into our own culture and time and place, but we should also try to place ourselves and our people *into* the Bible. It is simply not enough to sling scriptural verses at people in order to expect a positive response. I find it quite extraordinary, for instance, that the good Christian people who put a lot of money into poster-displays of biblical texts seem to be so worried about the imagined threat of modern translations of the Bible that they throw an early seventeenth-century version at unbelievers, expecting there to be positive communication. In the grace of God, some people do respond, even to this technique; but it is impossible to assess how many more become confirmed in their view that the Christian faith is totally out-of-date and irrelevant to today. When I travel to London on the train, at one of the stops I often find myself staring out of the carriage at a bright orange poster with the words 'REPENT YE, AND BELIEVE THE GOSPEL' (Mark 1:15). I respect the motives of those who paid for that poster, but I grieve at the fact that the message it is trying to convey is the very opposite of the one which is being read by the majority of passers-by.

These communication principles apply just as much to the preacher in the pulpit; our teaching about God from the Bible must be applied to life and culture as it is now, in the same way that it must speak the language we speak now. We read in Matthew 11:20–24:

> The people in the towns where Jesus had performed most of his miracles did not turn from their sins, so he reproached those towns. 'How terrible it will be for you, Chorazin! How terrible for you too, Bethsaida! If the miracles which were performed in you had been performed in Tyre and Sidon, the people there would long ago have put on sackcloth and sprinkled ashes on themselves, to show that they had turned from their sins! I assure you that on the Judgement Day God will show more mercy to the people of Tyre and Sidon than to you! And as for you, Capernaum!...'

It would be quite easy for us (especially those of us with Celtic blood) simply to go on about what a hard and unrepentant town Chorazin was, or how unbelieving was Bethsaida, how wicked were Tyre and Sidon, how miserable was Capernaum, how damnable was Sodom, and we would leave our people with a warm assurance that they're not like that! Or, if it's right to do so, we could put our people *in*

Chorazin and let them feel their own hardness of heart at the ministry of Jesus, and hear his condemnation of their stubborn self-reliance.

This putting of the people of God *into* the Bible need not only rebuke, it can bring comfort, encouragement, hope, and strength as well. The Bible is a vehicle of communication—its job is to bring the truth of God to mankind and mankind to God's truth. The Bible is God's own revelation of himself, and the God we worship is not some pagan deity, high and separated from a soiled world, but the God who has got his hands dirty in a stable at Bethlehem, in a carpenter's shop at Nazareth, pierced with the nails of a cross outside Jerusalem. Our God, unlike so many of us who are his people, will not separate the sacred from the secular, the pious from the profane; he abhors our religious hypocrisy. When God seeks to convey himself to us in the written and the preached Word, he wants to bring that word into every part of our existence, and every part of our existence can be brought into the Word. I once heard that great preacher, James Stewart, remind a group of future clergy that Christ took flesh 'so we have no right to disembody the gospel'. The gospel is embodied when we help our people to get into it.

When we preach biblically, we are not engaging in some technical exercise, some honourable tradition, some sacred habit—we long to bring the Word of the Lord to our people and to put our people into the Word of the Lord. Charles Smyth ended his book, *The Art of Preaching*, with these words:

> I wish that we all could preach—and I have known men who have done it—with as much earnestness, as much zeal, as much prophetic fervour, as though the Word of God which we are feebly trying to utter in our sermons were verily and indeed the most urgent and the most important thing in all the world: because, of course, it is.[11]

BUT HOW...?

There are many ways of preaching biblically; too often we drift into habits of preparing sermons which are easy and comfortable, picking up some verse which strikes us from the readings of the day, or latching on to some phrase which stuck in our minds from last Wednesday's Bible reading. But even the best of preachers needs to vary the way in which he approaches the Scriptures in his preaching. Nearly two hundred years ago, Charles Simeon criticised preachers who 'too often take routine texts which they may easily prate about, but comparatively seldom choose texts which require study and thinking over.'[12]

One can preach on a biblical theme. We might consider a series of sermons on Christian stewardship (or 'management' as it ought surely to be known, since we don't come across a lot of stewards these days—except, perhaps, on the racecourse!): 'Faithful with time,... with money,... with the gospel,... with witness,... to death', and so on. Or we could take a number of important biblical theme-words such as repentance, faith, love, hope, joy, peace, and so on.

One can preach on a broad sweep of the Bible. A series of sermons could be preached on the Passion and Resurrection stories in the four Gospels; or an outline series could be undertaken on the history of Israel from Samuel to Solomon. People who are hooked on the relatively modern tradition of preaching from a single verse or part of a verse can sometimes find this kind of preaching a bit unnerving but they end up with a better map to guide them in their own understanding of the Scriptures.

One can preach from a biblical story. The obvious stories are the parables of Jesus and of the Old Testament prophets. Some preachers have a remarkable inability to preach from a story, which they dismiss in a brief summary and then return to wallow in one verse. One might consider telling the story of Jonah or the ancient tale of Job (Job chapters

1–2 and 42). There are other stories, real life events, the first and last teaching-sermons of Jesus, in the Nazareth synagogue and on the Emmaus road, for instance, or the extended controversy between Peter and Paul reflected in Acts and Galatians, or the conversion of Saul of Tarsus (being careful to avoid the welcoming trap of just relating a few facts about Saul's life and a few comments on the later significance of the apostle Paul, then pouncing on the moment of his conversion in Acts 9:4–5). The preacher must learn the art of story-telling—an important part of any teaching ministry.

One can preach on a section of the Bible. For instance, sermons on each of the three so-called 'comforters' of Job and on Job himself would examine quite large sections of the book, revealing the main themes of the whole book; a sermon on a section of one of the New Testament letters, such as Ephesians 2:11–22 (the unity of all races in Christ) would attempt to search out God's word in Paul's whole argument. The same temptation arises to fasten onto a single verse and so to ignore the whole; it is the easy way out and it is simply unfair to the author. Often there is a focal verse, but if there is not, the preacher who fixes his attention on one part and ignores the whole is guilty of first degree pre-texting.

One can preach on biblical characters. Genesis and the early chapters of Exodus, for example, are full of very important characters, each of whom can illuminate our Christian lives, as can so many in the Old and New Testaments. It's a good idea to make a point of looking at some of the less important figures, and not to forget that many great saints of God have quite a few dirty panes in their stained glass!

One can preach from a verse. This has been the so-called 'normal' way of preaching in our culture for some time. We may have to choose the translation from which we take our verse with some care, to express what we believe was intended, and there are times when we will want to cross the boundaries between verses (chapters and verses are not part of the original text) in order to find the most appropriate and memorable form of the text. However, we must be careful to preach *from* the text and not *to* the text:

> Even if we know better than to use a text merely as a convenient peg on which to hang a sermon, and, at that, a peg which is sometimes not even selected until after the sermon has been written, still it is true that even our best and most successful sermons often ride very loosely to their texts.[13]

This very dangerous trap is one into which many preachers unconsciously fall when tackling a small text. The doctoring of texts has also been known: a mediaeval preacher is on record as speaking about the death of Archbishop Thomas Becket from the text, 'They killed the priest in front of the altars' (II Kings 11:18), without choosing to notice the whole text: 'They killed *Mattan*, the priest of *Baal*, in front of the altars'![14]

One can preach from a phrase or a word. There are a number of excellent Bible word-books available as a resource for the preacher searching out why John calls Jesus and the Holy Spirit, 'the paraclete' (I John 2:1; John 14:16 and 26; John 15:26; John 16:7), or how and why Mark so freely sprinkles his Gospel with 'immediately', or what Paul meant by 'the secret'. Perhaps some of the contrasts and paradoxes in biblical teaching could be explored, such as Paul's 'But now...' sayings (Romans 3:20–21; Romans 6:21–22; Ephesians 2:12–13; I Corinthians 15:9–10 and 19–20).

I want to emphasise the need for preachers to break out of the prison of always expounding a single verse or phrase, since there are so many people who think that it's the only proper kind of sermon! Preaching from a verse is as proper as any other kind of biblical preaching, but it is by no means the only way to preach biblically. If you look at the sermons in the Acts, you find almost no evidence for one-versing. Chapter 2 contains Peter's extended discourse on Joel 2:28—32 and Psalm 16:8–11, with references to other familiar parts of the Scriptures, but the heart of his message is the whole story of Jesus of Nazareth from the time of his ministry until that moment, the day of Pentecost. Chapter 7 gives us a lengthy account of the sermon by Stephen which clearly incensed his persecutors, though it was basically the story of the people of Israel, to which the betrayal and murder of God's righteous Servant were added at the very end. In chapter 8, Philip finds the Ethiopian reading the fourth servant song of Isaiah (Isaiah 52:13—53:12, though Luke cites merely Isaiah 53:7–8) and Philip expands on this section of Old Testament teaching to introduce the story of the Gospel of Jesus. Chapter 10 gives us a picture of Peter explaining the Christian Gospel to Cornelius and his relatives and friends, telling the story of Jesus from his baptism to his resurrection. In chapter 13, as we have already noticed, Paul preached in the synagogue at Pisidian Antioch by summarising the story of the people of Israel from the Egyptian exodus to the anointing of King David, linking this story to Jesus as the Son of David. In chapter 28, under house-arrest in Rome, Paul engages in dialogue-preaching, ranging over the whole of the Old Testament in an attempt to convince others about Jesus. Verse-preaching is *not* the only form of biblical preaching, nor is there any 'norm'.

'Contemporising'

The preacher has the whole of the Bible from which to find his message: he is not confined to the Gospels, nor to the New Testament, though all that he says is bound to be conditioned by the knowledge of God in Christ. It is one of God's curious coincidences that the obvious opening-place of our Bibles, between the testaments, is the point at which Christ's birth is announced, a symbol of the truth that he is the full and personal revelation of God, and the Saviour for all time to whom the Old Testament looks forward and the

New Testament looks at. Yet I find that I have preached few sermons on the latter chapters of Exodus and the books of Leviticus and Numbers, and I doubt whether I would be very proud of myself if I had preached hundreds from there! Most of those and other tough parts of the Old Testament I regard, in practice, as providing important background for those parts of the Scriptures which come to the foreground in the Gospel. It is as though some parts of the Bible are the stage scenery, in front of which the drama of the Gospel is acted out by a large cast of actors, each with a rôle to play, some more centrally than others. John Bright asks of our attitude to the Bible: 'Do we mean that it has authority once suitable exceptions have been made? But, in that event, who shall have the authority to say what those exceptions shall be?'[15] How can a Christian learn, he asks rhetorically, from the biblical heroes who lust and brawl and plot and kill? What of the vengefulness and hatred and lack of forgiveness in some of the Psalms? And how are we to comprehend the deeds of violence and bloodshed performed at the express command of God—the butchery of the entire Canaanite population, the extermination of the Amalekites, the stoning to death of the man who gathered sticks on the Sabbath? Bright goes on:

> What pastor has not heard the questions: 'But is God really like that? How do you reconcile such things with the teachings of Jesus?' They are fair questions. And whoever asks them has—whether he is aware of the fact or not—raised the problem of the authority of the Old Testament. He wants to know in what way such narratives can contribute to the Christian's understanding of his God, and how they can furnish guidance for Christian conduct. Nor will it do to turn the question aside with an easy answer, for it is clear that whatever authority such passages possess, they do not provide the Christian with examples which his God wishes him to imitate. Are we, after all, to advocate the

death penalty for those who absent themselves from church in order to pick up sticks—well, golf sticks at any rate—on Sunday? Is the church to deal with its foes by butchering them in the name of Christ? Christ forbids it! Are we, then, to regard such things as but examples of human fanaticism and ignorance or, alternatively, as actions which may have been necessary at the time but which are in no way to be imitated by us? But, in that event, wherein is their authority?[16]

Every pastor has heard the questions and has heard good Christians seeking to answer them. Too often our anwers carefully avoid the inevitable implications of the apparent divine command to slaughter a nation. The problem is that we are sometimes too concerned to protect the authority of the Bible, and our replies sound to the audience short on evidence, as though we sense that our doctrine of biblical authority was so insecure that it needs protecting! This escapism bothers me because I want to make positive affirmations about the scriptural word of God, but I am convinced that the doctrine is too tight a fit.

The sharp edges of the Old Testament and the (far fewer) sharp edges of the New must be interpreted fairly, in the light of biblical history, and must be read with Christian eyes. It is the overarching theology, the whole view of God and man and the world in the Scriptures, which is at the heart of their authority—the slaughter of the Amalekites is *part* of that view, not the whole of it, nor can it be detached from 'I am the good shepherd' (John 10:11). Bright concludes:

Having determined the theology that informs his text, the preacher must—because he is a Christian and has received the Old Testament from the hands of Christ, who is its fulfilment—bring his text to the New Testament, as it were, for verdict. He must ask what the New Testament has done with this aspect of the Old

Testament faith in the light of Christ... But... he does not for that reason leave his text behind and rush hastily on to preach a New Testament message. That would not be to preach from the Old Testament. Rather, he preaches from the Old Testament text itself —this very word in its plain meaning—but in the light of what its theology has become in Christ.[17]

There is no reason to suppose that all preaching that is biblical has to be based upon some announced biblical text, or theme, or story, for—in the end—it is not the Bible we preach, not a paper and ink idol, but Christ. The Bible is, in the words of Martin Luther, 'the cradle that bears the Babe of Bethlehem to us';[18] it is not the Babe himself. To preach in a way that is fully informed by the Scriptures and thoroughly consistent with them, yet taking as its subject some non-biblical theme, should not be censured as unbiblical. In Acts 17, Paul preaches at Athens about an altar he has seen 'To an Unknown God' on a text from Epimenides of Crete, and, in the last chapters of The Acts, Paul bases his preaching, to a hostile crowd and to Festus, Agrippa and Bernice, on his own testimony rather than a scriptural text. In our own time, there will be occasions when it is right to speak biblically about some important public issue, or about aspects of public morality, or to preach from the rich treasure of Christian biography. Let's imagine you are called to preach for a civic occasion when it's likely that a significant majority of the congregation has not been near a church for a year, except for something religious at Christmas. Any text you throw at the congregation from the Bible will carry no weight; but, if you begin where they are and lead them by a biblical path to Christ, you may get somewhere.

The preacher will be enabled to speak biblically of secular 'texts' as he develops a biblical mind, and it is only by the daily reading, meditating and study of the Bible that this can be achieved. Charles Simeon's advice is good: 'If we made a practice of selecting daily some short portion of Scripture for our meditation throughout the day, the most ignorant among us would soon obtain a knowledge which at present appears far beyond his reach.'[19] The continual refreshing of the preacher's mind from the whole of the Scriptures will be the most important factor in influencing his preaching biblically, preventing him from serving up what James Stewart has called 'great slabs of doctrine from the refrigerator of the preacher's mind'![20]

The biblical preacher is fundamentally one who brings the past witness of the Bible into the present day—he is, to use a frightful word, a contemporiser. We may be familiar with this technique in retelling the parables: no injustice is done to the text of Luke 10:29–37 in saying that the man on the Jericho road was mugged, that he was avoided by a pastor or a priest or a lay preacher, that the good Samaritan used antiseptic and band-aids, and that he drove a car to take him to hospital—none of those changes affects the principle of the story. Further, in circumstances where there is sectarian hatred, the point of the story will be strengthened if the two men are identified as being on opposite sides of a Protestant/Roman Catholic or Christian/Muslim divide. R H Mounce described preaching as 'the medium through which God contemporises His historic self-disclosure in Christ, and offers man the opportunity to respond in faith'. It is the privilege of the preacher to contemporise what he finds in the Bible, bringing the Bible to the present day and placing today's people into the Bible.

Translating

The preacher is also a translator. At its most obvious level, this means he is a trader in language and must have profound respect for the language he uses. David Read told the story of a professor of theology at a Korean mission who began an address, 'In our approach to ultimate reality we tend to proceed either inductively or deductively,'[21] translated as, 'I am here to tell you what Jesus Christ means to me.' It sounds as if no-one was listening! But the preacher is bound also to be involved in the process of translating from Hebrew and Greek, the original languages of the Bible. The majority of us who preach have little or no knowledge of Hebrew, and our knowledge of Greek can be pretty rusty, so we rely on commentaries to provide us with additional assistance. Apart from the critical questions of grammar in a few crucial places, the most important aspect of translating language is to know what the same word would have meant to the same audience in a different context, normally outside the Christian Church.

For example, in John 1:12 the word we normally translate 'receive' means, in other contexts, to grasp eagerly, as a drowning man might grasp a plank floating in the water. Two verses later, in John 1:14, the expression we normally translate 'lived among us' means 'pitched his tent among us'. Bible translators are familiar with this process in reverse: the Bible Society tells of the equatorial Karré people and their difficulty in translating 'the Comforter/Helper'. They found an excellent phrase in the custom of a line of porters carrying heavy loads on their heads: if one porter is exhausted and another sees him lying on the ground, stoops down and supports him, he is known as 'the one who falls down beside us', a superb equivalent.

Pure biblical literalism has become the rallying cry of some Christian groups and there seems to me to be a lemming-like desire among them to outdo one another in exaggeration, and yet that kind of approach to the Bible is almost the opposite of the Bible's own view of itself as the living, active, penetrating and effective word of the Lord.

There are some modern versions of the Bible which are so obsessive about the literal rendering of each word that they miss the basic point: translation is the transfer of *meaning*. You cannot translate meaning without taking the context at each end of the process into account; too few preachers and translators take the context at the receiving end, at our end, seriously enough. Arguably the greatest individual translator of this century was J B Phillips. He described his aim as:

> not one hundred percent accuracy, which is impossible in any case, but at its equivalent effect. That is to say, he will try to reproduce in today's hearers and readers the same emotions as were produced by the original documents so long ago. This, to my mind, is a very difficult, but not hopelessly impossible objective... If we are to be successful translators we cannot afford to be detached.[22]

This dynamic way of translating meaning in order to produce equivalent effect is the job of the preacher as well. Helmut Thielicke has drawn our attention to the fact that the work of translation begins with the text in its original language and, at the preacher's end, it 'means that I must tell the old story and put it in the language of today. And this must be done repeatedly;... But translating means more than a mere recasting in words. It means making "relevant" too, so that the hearer remarks, "Why, that has to do with me!"'[23]

THE ART OF EXEGESIS

But how, in practice, does the preacher go about his task of bringing the Bible to the people and putting the people into the Bible? He must begin by allowing the text (in whatever sense he's using the term) to set the agenda for the sermon. But how is this agenda to be found? There is a basic art to biblical exegesis (that is, explaining the text and interpreting its meaning), and it can be listed in five simple stages.

Stage one: look at the text. Apart from simply reading the text, which—in the case of a story—may take quite a long time, look at it with fresh eyes and ask yourself what it meant when it was written and what it means to you in its unexplained form now. In the first place, always prefer the simplest reading of the text; you may have to modify your thinking later.

Stage two: determine the context. Where does the text come from in the history and literature of God's people? And what kind of literature is it—historical, poetic, liturgical, a letter, a gospel or what?

Stage three: examine the intention of the writer. It is important to remember that a 'text means what its author meant.'[24] It may mean more, but it cannot mean less. Martin Luther wrote that good theologians take the Bible in 'the single, proper, original sense, the sense in which it is written... The Holy Spirit is the simplest writer and speaker in heaven and earth.'[25] John Calvin (1509–1564) wrote the same: 'It is the first business of an interpreter to let his author say what he does say, instead of attributing to him what we think he ought to say.'[26]

Stage four: expose the meaning. That is, find the simplest means of revealing what it is saying. This cannot be taught, for every text is different. But be careful! I was taken quite by surprise when I heard a trainee lay preacher interpret Matthew 8:19–20 ('Foxes have holes, and birds have nests, but the Son of Man has nowhere to lie down and rest') as a request for a bed for the night!

Stage five: apply the text to life. This is what the old writers used to call 'vitalising'—bringing to life. Having done all the preparatory work to discover what the text means, this is the point at which the people are brought to the Bible.

During this process, the preacher will have read commentaries (and made sure that he retains his own judgement), he will have noted the insights which have been given him as he has read the text, and he will look at other scriptures. Then, with a page or two of scribblings in front of him, he will look for possible headings and a clear structure. What he is looking for is the simplest means of conveying his message. John Wyclif was keen on simplicity: 'O, if the Apostle had heard such hair-splitting, how he must have despised it!'[27] He might want to look for an overall aim for the sermon, though I am completely convinced that the setting of an aim should be left to the very end of the preparation so that it is derived and not imposed. At this stage, the preacher should, in the words of Simeon,

> mark the *character* of the passage (for example, decla-
> ration, precept, promise, invitation, appeal, etc.).
> Mark the *spirit* of the passage (it may be tender and
> compassionate, or indignant and menacing; but
> whatever it be, let that be the spirit of your dis-
> course...).[28]

The preacher who seeks to bring together his audience and the Scriptures acts under divine command and authority and is responsible to God for the way he discharges that trust.

> He speaks as a teacher and advocate of the Christian
> gospel—nothing else. Indeed, there is fundamentally
> no other reason that he should speak at all, and cer-
> tainly none that the faithful should trouble to listen to
> him... His task, then, is to expound the Christian gos-
> pel, to summon his hearers to accept that gospel and to
> live in a manner consonant with it.[29]

The basis of his own preaching is the divine authority of the Scriptures, and he himself is subject to that same authority. Not only is the minister sent by God to his task, but he brings God's word in human speech. There is a common misunderstanding among many congregations that preachers speak out of their own experience. Though experience is, no doubt, of value, it does not constitute the basis of authority in preaching and can lead to spiritual arrogance: younger preachers can imagine that their new discoveries of truth are unknown to older Christians, and older preachers can be patronising, giving the impression that they have learned and know it all. Two great nineteenth-century evangelical preachers, Joseph Parker and Charles Spurgeon, had a public disagreement, and

Parker took his brother to task: 'The universe is not divided into plain black and white as you suppose... Believe me, you really are not infallible.'[30] However good our intentions may be, when we stray from the divine authority of the Bible, we are not infallible! The preacher, therefore, needs to be very careful about the unwritten text which comes across from his preaching, his cultural and, perhaps even class prejudices, and the temptations of arrogance.

The preacher of the Bible needs to be a man or woman of intellectual and spiritual integrity. This is very much easier when we have a trusted Christian friend, relation or colleague who can be perceptive and critical without being hurtful. My wife, Pauline, was trained as a theologian, so I don't have to go very far for the content of my preaching and my own integrity to be tested! I am also very thankful for a five-year curacy under the authority of a vicar who challenged many of my false moves (lots of those!) and refused to let me get away with prejudiced, half-digested or unjustifiable rubbish in the pulpit. As we get older, we find it more difficult to take honest criticism; if we are not exposed to it at an early stage in our ministries, we who preach will be seriously deprived. Though the preacher speaks words which, because they belong to the Bible, are not entirely his own, he is not at liberty to utter words which he would not be willing to defend. He has no right to stand in the pulpit and to prattle on about things he does not believe and has no intention of practising. 'Be also very careful,' wrote Richard Baxter, 'that you preach to yourselves the sermons that you study, before you preach them to others.'[31] The preacher who relies entirely on his rôle, without any conviction that what he says is true, ought to stop preaching, for his own sake and for the sake of his people.

The preacher will find it necessary to develop a system of doctrine which responds to his reading of the Bible and which gives him a theological filing cabinet and a tidy mind. Christian doctrines have an annoying but invariable habit of behaving like wooden building-blocks. If you take one away, you may knock over the next one and dislodge a few others as well!

Take the ancient controversy over whether human beings are eternally predestined or are free to make real and lasting choices at will—an argument which, I guess, highly delights the devil. Those who are totally convinced about the predestination block will probably shift the block which describes our need of prayer and the block which describes God as absolute love; those who are equally convinced about the freedom of the human will block are likely to move the block which teaches the omnipotence of God's grace and the block which refuses to let us describe faith as an achievement; those who try to stack together the two doctrinal blocks notice that it's very difficult because both blocks have now lost their shape; and those who hold on to both doctrinal blocks, one in each hand as a Christian paradox, are accused of inconsistency or being incapable of building with the blocks. You can't win! Without some awareness of doctrinal shapes and relationships, the preacher is likely to lead his congregation into any number of difficulties.

By the concept of a system, I do not mean a pattern into which the Bible is forced to fit, but an understanding of where one biblical doctrine is in relation to another, where they touch and, to change the analogy, even merge. I remember clearly a good sermon on Psalm 73 (the righteous man's envy of the wicked man), in which verses 18– 20 and 27—'They [the wicked] are instantly destroyed; they go down to a horrible end', etc—were explained in terms of the doctrine of eternal punishment. Hell was justified (and I recall the words) in terms of God 'honouring man's decision to rebel against him'. I wonder why he had not honoured *my* decision to rebel against him (for, like all mankind, I have rebelled). Why was Saul of Tarsus saved when he had made a firm commitment against Jesus? A goodly number of other doctrinal building-blocks were toppled or wobbled dangerously! A proper examination of eternal punishment must be related to the doctrine of God, his justice, his mercy, his holiness and his love.

The preacher also needs to keep in his mind or, at least, on his bookshelf and within reach of his mind, a knowledge of where to go in the Bible for important evidence of various doctrines, and to be willing to face up to the parts of the biblical evidence that go counter to his own understanding. Take that tough doctrine of hell, again. In the first place, the first three Gospels and some of the other New Testament books give clear evidence for the doctrine of eternal punishment—Jesus himself accepts the classic illustration of Jerusalem's rubbish dump, Gehenna (see Matthew 5:22 and 29–30; Mark 9:43; Luke 10:15, etc).

The apostle John, on the other hand, writes of the same eternal issues in terms of life and death, not of heaven and hell (see John 3:15–16; 5:21–26; 6:50; 8:21 and 51; 10:28; 11:25–26; I John 2:25; 3:14; 4:19; 5:11–20; and many more)—as also does Paul (Romans 6:23 and elsewhere). In contrast to both, there are a few verses in Saint Paul's letters which do more than hint at universal salvation (see Romans 8:12–13; 11:25–36; I Corinthians 15:22, Colossians 1:20); there are also hints each way (Romans 9:19–29 and 11:16–24); and there are texts which assume the doctrine of hell (Galatians 1:8 and 9; Philippians 3:19; I Thessalonians 2:3). It simply will not do to decide on the doctrine of hell (because it's more convenient for evangelism), and to explain that, in Saint John's many references, he must have meant hell when he wrote about death, excusing Saint Paul's universalist references by intricate exegesis and by churning out some jargon which means, in effect, that the teaching of the Synoptic Gospels is normal so these verses must be made to conform! Naturally, preaching and theology go together but it is preaching which comes first: the Bible is the product of the preaching of God's people, whether it be the ancient stories told from generation to generation, or the records of prophetic preaching, or the story of the Preacher from Nazareth, or the preaching of the first

Christians, or the written sermons of the apostles. Helmut
Thielicke writes:

> I am convinced that preaching has primacy over theol-
> ogy, and that theology merely works back to investigate
> the basis of that which it has already heard proclaimed.
> It seems to me to be a perversion when contemporary
> theology is regarded... as an undertaking which first
> must investigate the possibility of preaching and lay
> down the conditions for it... The fact is that the prim-
> ary decisions are reached in the preaching, where the
> active Word becomes Event. Here is where the great
> theological themes begin to take shape.[32]

Fundamentally, the preacher must have a basic grasp of
the central truths of the faith, how they fit together and
where they come from in the Bible; scholars tell us that there
are five key themes which appear throughout the sermons
recorded in the Acts of the Apostles, the first and second
being absolutely crucial to all the preaching. The first
emphasis is on the death of Christ; the second is the Resurrection and heavenly reign of Christ; the third is Jesus as the
fulfilment of the Old Testament hopes of the Messiah; the
fourth and lightest emphasis is on the earthly life and ministry of Jesus; the fifth, personal emphasis is on repentance
and faith. The preacher who is not convinced of these basics
of the Gospel is not in a position to fulfil his ministry. 'No-
body,' wrote James Denney in a commentary on II Corinthians, 'has any right to preach who has not mighty affirmations to make concerning God's Son Jesus Christ—affirmations about which there is no ambiguity.'[33]

However, let us not, in our respect for the Bible, regard it
as a germ-free environment, totally sanitised by our sterile
veneration, for it will then become useless and ineffective. It
is unfortunately the case that most Christian people prefer a
hygienic Bible and antiseptic doctrine which leave them
with no stray germs, no important unanswered questions,

which exalt their biblical heroes beyond reproach—just try suggesting that Saint Paul may have been a trifle arrogant and watch the sparks fly! We must take the risk of letting the unsanitised Bible speak as it is.

If Parson Snuffle wants to explain simply why he preaches from the Bible, it is because he has a longing to preach nothing but Christ, the living Word. J G Davies wrote: '...to preach Christianity and to preach Christ are not identical—the one is a system of thought and practice, the other is the revelation of a person.'[34] Christian faith is wholly personal. It is not a matter of how much you know but of *Whom* you know and love. This kind of faith in God is never secure, rarely cut and dried, for it is all about relationships, and relationships are always as difficult as they are satisfying. 'Life would be OK without people,' we say with a smile in our parish office during one of those days, but, of course, we wouldn't want to be without them. At times, life with the living God can be quite disturbing, but we wouldn't find life with a rule book or a *Teach Yourself Getting to Know God* very fulfilling!

John Newton (1725–1807) had a 'grand point' in all his preaching: 'to break the hard heart and to heal the broken one', or (to bring it up to date) 'to comfort the disturbed and disturb the comfortable'![35] Faithful biblical preaching will inevitably do that. Martin Luther said he preached to the servants and the children, 'And if the learned men are not well pleased with what they hear, well, the door is open.'[36] The preaching of the living Word through the Scriptures, bringing the Bible to today's hearers and placing them into the Bible, can have a powerful effect if only more who preach and more who hear would realise it. It will not often be popular—whoever said it would be?—and, though it will meet many of our people's deepest needs, it won't always meet them all; it should not bring us success and it may give us some heartaches. But Jesus said, 'Whoever loses his life for my sake will gain it' (Matthew 10:39).

NOTES

[1] Douglas Bush, ed *The Essential Milton* (Viking: London, 1949), from *Samson Agonistes*, lines 300–306, p 622.

[2] D F Strauss, *The Life of Jesus Critically Examined* translated by George Eliot (1846), ed from the second English edition by P C Hodgson (SCM: London, 1973).

[3] Lakeland: Basingstoke, 1984, pp 19 and 20.

[4] Donald Coggan, *The Ministry of the Word* (Lutterworth: London, 1964), p 78.

[5] Tr E B Pusey, *The Confessions of Saint Augustine* (Dent: London, 1907), Book 8, [12] 29, p 171.

[6] O Scheel, *Dokumente zu Luthers Entwicklung (bis 1519)*, p 191. See E G Rupp and B Drewery, ed *Martin Luther* (Edward Arnold: London, 1970), p 6.

[7] G Offor, ed *The Works of John Bunyan* (Edinburgh: 1862), 3 vols.

[8] Nehemiah Curnock, ed *John Wesley's Journal* (Epworth: London, 1949) pp 36–7n, 45, 51.

[9] *The General Instruction on the Roman Missal*, paragraph 9.

[10] SCM: London, 1967, p 162.

[11] Charles Smyth, *The Art of Preaching 747–1939* (SPCK: London, 1940), p 247.

[12] Quoted from Simeon's sermon classes by H E Hopkins, *Charles Simeon of Cambridge* (Hodder and Stoughton: London, 1977), p 88.

[13] Smyth, *op cit*, p 45.

[14] Thomas Waley, *De Modo Componendi Sermones cum Documentis*, quoted from Charles Smyth *ibid*, p 97.

[15] John Bright, *op cit*, p 55.

[16] *ibid*, p 60.

[17] *ibid*, pp 211–212.

[18] E T Bachman, ed *Luther's Works* (Fortress: Philadelphia, 1960), vol 35, pp 123 and 236 (*A Brief Instruction on... the Gospels* and *Preface to the Old Testament*).

[19] Charles Simeon, *Horae Homileticae* (1833), Sermon 2187.

[20] James Stewart, Durham *Pastoral Theology* lectures 1970.

[21] David Read, *The Lyman Beecher Lecture*, 1974 in *Sent from God: the Enduring Power and Mystery of Preaching* (Abingdon: 1974), pp 106–7.

[22] J B Phillips, *The Price of Success* (Hodder and Stoughton: London, 1984), pp 151 and 153.

[23] Helmut Thielicke, *How Modern Should Theology Be?* tr H G Anderson (Collins Fontana: Great Britain, 1967), p 8.

[24] E D Hirsch, *Validity in Interpretation* (Yale University: 1967), p 1.

[25] R C Johnson, *Authority in Protestant Theology* (Westminster: Philadelphia, 1959), p 29.

[26] F W Farrar, *The History of Interpretation* (Baker: Grand Rapids, Michigan, 1961), p 347.

[27] H B Workman, *John Wyclif: A Study of the English Mediaeval Church* (1926), vol 2, p 212, quoted from Charles Smyth *op cit*, p 54.

[28] Charles Simeon, *Horae Homileticae op cit*, vol 21, p 330.

[29] John Bright, *op cit*, p 21.

[30] *Open Letter from Joseph Parker to Charles Spurgeon*, 1890, from W Adamson, *The Life of the Rev Joseph Parker* (Glasgow, 1902), and quoted from David Edwards, *Christian England* vol 3 (Collins/Fount: Glasgow, 1984), pp 261–262.

[31] Richard Baxter, *The Reformed Pastor*, ed J T Wilkinson (Epworth: London, 1939), written originally in 1655.

[32] Helmut Thielicke, *op cit*, p 85.

[33] James Denney, *The Second Epistle to the Corinthians* (Hodder and Stoughton: London).

[34] J G Davies, *Worship and Mission* (SCM Press: London, 1966).

[35] John Newton, in J C Pollock, *Amazing Grace* (Hodder and Stoughton: London, 1981), p 155.

[36] See especially E T Bachmann *op cit*, vol 51, for Luther on Preaching.

Chapter 6

KEEPING IN TOUCH: The Way it Used to Be

It might have been all right if he hadn't agreed to a new Ladies' Knitting and Fellowship Circle banner for the Church! That's when the rumours began to fly and the general grumblings all came to the surface. The Ladies' Circle— or the Granny Club as it was known to the younger members of Saint Guthlac's Church—had been founded in the late 1920s, and one of its first acquisitions was a banner. This was, in itself, a period piece, but it had seen better days; the wooden frame was still intact but the fabric was falling apart. The threads were dangling off and if anyone had dared to have it dry-cleaned, there wouldn't have been much left at the end!

Now the Granny Club had been infiltrated by younger women who thought they were doing everyone a favour by offering to replace the fabric on the banner. Everyone seemed happy—everyone, that is, except Mrs Honeysuckle, the secretary (generally, in church groups as in the Communist world, it is the secretaries who wield the real power!). Portia Honeysuckle did not agree, and she had lots of friends on the fringes of the church who were only too delighted to take up her cause. Before he knew it—and most of the congregation knew before *he* knew it—poor Parson Snuffle was cast in the rôle of the villainous radical, sweeping away all that was good and comforting in the past for the sake of modernity! Everywhere he went in the village, it seemed, people were giving him strange looks, and gentle, kindly souls were recommending some easy compromise 'for peace sake'.

Perhaps our pastor should have acted sooner to quench

the flames, because before long he had a forest fire on his hands. That tatty piece of half-century-old fabric (about which letters were passing backwards and forwards to people in authority almost daily) had become a symbol for all the deeper complaints about Mr Snuffle's ministry (you remember that he had not been in the area for very long), especially the grievances of the folk who didn't go to church any more and didn't like the look of the new ones who did. That banner was another symptom of the modernising of religion—and there is nothing that a very religious person hates more than the present day!

The services have been modernised, the prayers are not often sprinkled with 'thees' and 'thous' any more; the cobweb that's been up in the corner over the pulpit since at least 1945 has been swept away; there's talk about giving money away, and even the parish magazine's had a facelift. But, when the truth comes out, it's the sermons which are at the root of the trouble because (despite all the parson's problems with his sermons) they're beginning to hit the target. Last month, for instance, he let an African pastor—and a woman, too!—preach at both the services; then he followed that up with some talk about proper giving to the overseas missionary societies, and that was guaranteed to get a lot of people very heated! 'He seems to think that we, the Church in Britain, of all places,' he heard someone say in the Post Office, 'we who invented Christianity, can learn from people in Africa and India and South America! Whoever heard of such a thing!' It took a lot of courage and determination (not something which Septimus Snuffle thought he had in him), lots of occupational deafness, and quite a few months to dampen down the flames of fringe-religion—'half-fidelity', as Burke called it.

The previous minister had been careful to avoid anything controversial, always keen to appease, never willing to make any painful changes that could possibly be deferred. His preaching was the same: gentle, classical little pieces which were careful to avoid anything which might cause his standing invitation to the quarterly sherry party with the local member of parliament at Squire Bufton-Smithers' to be withdrawn. I suppose the establishment was his chief sin, but he had known of other preachers who were equally afraid of their lay leadership (after all, they controlled the money); some of them had to be even more careful in the pulpit than he was. His sermon illustrations were all drawn from the same places: from 'my period of army service in Egypt during the last war' or 'as Plato once remarked', and never once did he raise so much as an eyebrow (cruel people might say he didn't raise many eyelids, either). But Parson Snuffle is different: he's ready to talk about what he's seen on television, he took issue with the council in the local paper about its school bus policy, and he talked about it in a sermon. He's been on about unemployment, and abortion, and all this about the Church abroad, and mission. It's not that the half-faithful don't like him or that they think he's a bad pastor; it's just that they wish he'd keep the pulpit away from the world. They have this curious idea that the Christian faith can exist in a kind of holy bubble, untouched by the world and not making contact with it. In short, Mrs Honeysuckle and her friends liked it the way it used to be.

... WITH THE PEOPLE

Any pastor-preacher knows that the effects of prophetic preaching can stretch well beyond the walls of the church and will come to the surface in a congregation—or even in a whole community in villages or self-contained housing estates—when it touches the people. Preaching that touches people can bring annoyance, offence, even division, but it can equally bring comfort, peace and guidance. It's a pattern which can be seen throughout the history of prophecy: the people to whom the message was sent did not always (in fact, not often) respond in the right way to the messenger, but, whether the word was one of condemnation or consolation, it is clear that the message itself touched the people. The parable of the tenants in the vineyard (Mark 12:1–12, etc) tells the story of the rejection of God's messengers and of the owner's own son; the tenants are thrown out at the end of the parable not because they failed to hear but because they failed to respond to the word.

The preacher today must not concern himself, in the first instance, with how his people will react: rather, he must make sure that his message gets through to them clearly. If they do not *respond*, that is their problem, but if they do not *hear*, that is his. When Jesus gave instructions to the 72 disciples that he sent on a preaching and healing mission (Luke 10:1–12) he told them to say the same thing to those who welcomed them as to those who rejected them: 'The Kingdom of God has come near you.' We shall never be able to measure response, but wherever the herald goes and touches people with his message, the Kingdom comes.

So preaching must make contact with people, and it is a very important duty of all preachers to keep in touch with people so that the message can be addressed to where people really are. Helmut Thielicke wrote:

> As long as I can discover no connection between the gospel and the problems of my life, then it has nothing to say to me and I am not interested. And that is precisely why the gospel must be preached afresh and told in new ways to every generation, since every generation has its own unique questions. This is why the gospel must constantly be forwarded to a new address, because the recipient is repeatedly changing his place of residence... In short, if the basic questions of life have shifted, then I must redirect the message of the gospel. Otherwise I am answering questions that have never been asked. And, upon hearing such answers, my opposite number will just shake his head and say, 'That's no concern of mine. It has nothing to do with me'.[1]

The job of preacher is to enable people to hear so that they can respond. To do that, he must keep himself in touch with his people and make his preaching relevant to them.

One answer to this problem is simply to say that if only you tell the story of the Bible as it is, people will hear a message that has no sell-by date on it so it won't go bad, and the only address it needs is the one it already has on it: 'To all mankind'. There is some truth in this, of course, but there is considerable culpable naïvety as well. The Bible which is just 'told as it is' is already in some translation—it may be old or it may be new, but it isn't pure. The person who 'tells it as it is' is not some disembodied being with no prejudices, no personality and no life history, and the same is true of the person to whom the story is told. God is perfectly well aware that his message always comes through human agency—if we fail to grasp that, we have been reading our Bible with extraordinary prejudice, for the God of the Bible is the God of relationships and personality. It was Phillips Brooks who wrote so wisely that all preaching is 'the communication of truth through personality'[2]: it is true of the Bible, and it is true of our preaching. Because the essential relationship between humanity and God is one based on faith (which is entirely personal) rather than law (which is usually non-personal), in the task of communicating God's Word to people, I cannot sufficiently emphasise the importance of rooting what we say in the lives of people, illustrated from their true experience, so that through it the Word of the personal Lord can be clearly heard.

One of the problems with the training of preachers is that it must, in the first instance, be theoretical. While a lot is being done in the sphere of application to practical ministry—pastoral studies, missiology, closer links with local churches, and the like—it is still an unfortunate fact that too many of those who train preachers have had less than five years' experience in church ministry. More teachers of preachers have had experience of industry, commerce or the dole, and that is all to the good, but too few of them have had enough time to reflect on ministry from the inside before trying to impart it to others. Related to that is the difficulty that many college teachers seem to be those who have ministered in the very untypical church with a large staff and a gathered, articulate congregation where all the wonderful theories of ministry come from. The task of earthing the Bible in realistic preaching begins with the training of preachers. Then, when the new preacher is licensed or ordained, he or she is too often given the impression of being 'qualified': competent to stand up in the pulpit and pronounce on the Bible and to issue infallible edicts on all manner of topics. I am firmly convinced that every preacher, lay or ordained, should be under the regular and critical guidance of a more experienced pastor. Apart from picking up the new preacher's silly faults, the experienced pastor will know better how to keep preaching in touch with the people.

W E Sangster, himself a very gifted and witty sermon illustrator, in *The Craft of Sermon Illustration*[3] outlined seven reasons for good sermon illustration: first, it can help to make the message clear; second, it gives the congregation a little breathing-space (a very prosaic but important reason); third, it can make truth visible, less commonplace and tedious; fourth, it can make the sermon interesting ('a tradition of dullness in preaching has developed in some circles and it seems almost to be taken as a mark of sanctity if the sermon is certain to bore!'); fifth, it helps people to remember what they have heard; sixth, it can help to persuade people; seventh, if skilfully used, it can help to recapitulate without a sense of repetition.

Jesus illustrated his message, as we have seen earlier, and many of the great preachers of the early centuries were keen illustrators—Ambrose and Augustine, for instance. In the middle ages, the Franciscan and Dominican preachers developed sermon illustration to such an extent that it almost took over from the message: they had special categories of illustration—biblical, pious, examples from the saints, visionary, classical, historical, legendary, those taken from fables, moralised allegories, personal anecdotes, and so on. This fondness for illustration was akin to much of the folk and ritual drama of the period, to the great passion play cycles and later religious works, to *Doctor Faustus, Paradise Lost* and *Pilgrim's Progress*. On the other hand, some of the greatest preachers have been known to use few means of illustration: Martyn Lloyd-Jones was exceedingly sparing with all but biblical illustrations, and John Stott over-modestly protests that he is 'trying to improve'![4] They must be the exceptions to the rule, and this book would not dare to pretend that it could be of any use to the likes of them, but more for the likes of simple folk like me. I need to illustrate, or I lose contact with people from the pulpit. But if I lose contact with people when I'm out of the pulpit, I won't be able to illustrate.

In what ways is the preacher to keep in touch so that his preaching can be properly illustrated and effective?

... WITH CONTEMPORARY THINKING

The preacher must spend time in study. The advice which often used to be given by senior clergy to those less experienced in the ministry is not often heard today: a proper amount of time spent in the study is not time wasted. We are inclined to rush around from a service to a hospital, to some sick visiting, to a funeral, to a school, to the duplicator, to a committee, to a prayer group, to a sermon, and so on. And we do not take any time to study. When we do, we feel guilty about it, as though we're not giving value for money while we sit and read. This is a message for non-preachers: give your preacher time to study, whether it is on some project or simply trying to get through that pile of unread books on his study mantelpiece which grows by two or three every year.

One of the most humbling and rewarding experiences of my ministry happened when I had been ordained about ten years and was due to meet what seemed an impossible deadline for a thesis I had foolishly undertaken some years earlier. The church treasurer arrived at my house just after lunch one Sunday to announce that he had contacted all the church councillors in each of the two churches and that I was to take a week's break from that moment to complete my library research; then I was to take a sabbatical period of three months during which my only duties were to be Sunday worship, hospital visiting and funerals. The rest, they would do. I realised afterwards that when the people of God have the right priorities they are willing to do much of the work which the ministry has kept to itself, and one of their best assets is a preacher or pastor who thinks. Don't let me give the impression that it's only the clergy who are busy— lay preachers are often just as pushed for time, and they need the opportunity to study just as much.

The preacher must read. It used to be said that preachers should always have four books on the go at any one time: the Bible, Shakespeare or one of the literary classics, something of personal interest, and a work of theology. Those were the days! I am sure this is expecting too much of preachers today, except in certain rare environments. However, the general principle is not a bad one: that the preacher should reflect in his reading as wide a scope as he can and also fulfil some of his own God-given interests. Our reading may cover works of literature (the classics and the off-beat), biography (hopefully something a little more meaty than the milk-and-water stuff that keeps most church bookstalls solvent), travel, the sciences and the world of nature, history and theology. If you are a scientist turned preacher, don't neglect your science as a study—and not just because you can use it to grind some theological axe. If you're an artist or an architect or a writer, do not assume that all these disciplines must be dissolved by the preaching. It's also important to keep an eye on newspapers and magazines. Although newspapers and periodicals are, of course, reading, because they are by nature very short-lived they are much more akin to our intake from television and radio than to the reading of books.

The preacher should keep in touch with television and

radio. Most ministers know the experience of going to visit a family, perhaps prior to a funeral; the telly is on. You're invited to sit down and you make a few remarks, but no one can hear you, so someone heads for the box. 'Aha!' you think, 'They're going to turn it off.' No such luck. It's just the volume that goes down and the big screen continues to flash its images at you. Something odd then begins to happen: the family doesn't notice the television (because it's as much a part of their sitting room as the wallpaper) but you can't keep your eyes off it and you start to drift off into a video-trance, until someone ask you if you're tired and you suddenly remember that you haven't really been listening! Count yourself happy that at least they turned down the volume!

You are, thankfully, not addicted to television: many people are totally hooked. You don't want to become a telly mainliner, but you ought to have some idea of what your congregation is watching and listening to, often for many hours a day (though churchgoers, as a general rule, are normally more sparing in their use of the on button than most). We watch and listen not so much to collect illustrative material as to put ourselves in the place that people find themselves. We may rightly hate the commercialisation of Christmas, for instance, but if we haven't noticed that the television commercials for Christmas toys started in mid-September, we may find ourselves speaking at the wrong moment. Of course, we watch and listen because we're interested, not simply because we're preachers!

There are, however, some thorny issues here: television is a notoriously corruptive infuence, partly because it is very convincing and we find it difficult to disbelieve it, partly because it immunises us to such things as violence, and partly because there are some nasty videos about. But it will not do if the preacher confines his intake to Christian records, religious and other programmes before 9 pm, wholesome Christian magazines and church newspapers; these won't help us to know where most people are most of the time.

I have three pet media dislikes: television soap operas (though I'm addicted to *The Archers* on radio), political question-and-discussion programmes on radio and television (because I get steamed up at the half-truths and party propaganda that keep up the ratings), and Saturday evening brassy quiz shows (which seem to me to degrade humanity to one of its lowest levels), but I cannot ignore them, nor the ethos each of them represents. Many people to whom I preach think they're the best programmes of the week, and no doubt they find my favourites equally distasteful. By keeping in touch, even with things I dislike, I can discover some of the best ways to speak relevantly to God's people.

It might also be helpful to observe how people view and hear the media. Not so long ago, it was virtually impossible, and certainly a bit dissolute, to watch the tube before lunchtime—indeed, in some circles, it might have seemed reprobate to switch it on before the evening news—but now many of us have become addicted to breakfast television. Not only has our pattern of viewing changed, but the way we view has changed. At one time, we watched intently or fell asleep in front of the screen, now, it's become more of a constant companion in many homes, always there but less often noticed. Things have changed since the time, not so very long ago, when at least half the population didn't have a television, that one of my schoolmasters told me that he could not concentrate on the wireless unless he was looking at it! Nowadays, electronic communication is part of our basic diet and, even if we lament the fact, we cannot avoid it. The people with whom preachers seek to communicate are, by and large, readers of newspapers which exist on black-and-white opinions, hearers of radio in the car, at work, in bed or over lunch—perhaps even in the betting shop! The overwhelming majority of them do not sit on wooden benches to listen to talks on abstract concepts delivered in cold buildings. We must come to terms with the way people hear the media—and, maybe even discover the way to help them listen.

Most trainee clergy have a brief opportunity to work with television and radio, and anyone who takes the trouble to enquire can fairly easily join a training course in understanding and using the media. Groups such as *Christian Communication* have been set up by those who are concerned that the Church should use all the resources available for communicating the Gospel, and many other agencies, like the Bible Society, in addition to the theological colleges and religious affairs departments of the broadcasting authorities are remarkably willing to help. This can do nothing but good.

The preacher must keep abreast of important local issues. In a unified community, it is much easier—and also more important—to keep in touch with local concerns: making sure you see the community council report, keeping in touch with the community policeman, establishing trusting relationships with pensioners' groups, and the like. You may get involved in issues about local schools, health services, care for the elderly, the closure of a Post Office or even the roadworks. In one of the parishes in which I served, I was drawn into a two-year community council's debate on the appropriate shape of kissing gates big enough for children's pushchairs.

The place where I serve now is at the opposite extreme: a parish that straddles about four distinct areas of Cardiff, like four slices of a huge cake and with a congregation drawn from across and beyond the city. To keep in touch with all the local issues here has to be the job of the congregation, and the more perceptive ones will keep their minister in touch with the big concerns.

There is a warning to be issued in dealing with local issues. It is very important not to use the pulpit in order to 'have your say' or even 'put people right' or, blasphemously, to get at people. A certain type of spouse can easily influence a preacher to make pointed comments which ought never to be made in the name of the Lord, and unmarried preachers can allow their unchecked emotions to get the better of them. All too easily, our prejudices show through when we are preaching and we leave our people in the frustrating position of being unable to answer back: in that frame of mind, all the preacher will do is create anger and undermine the authority of the word.

The preacher is a pastor. Charles Smyth wrote truly:

> The man of average gifts and average abilities is not enabled to preach the Word of God with power if he be isolated from the rough and tumble of a pastoral ministry: for it is precisely in the whole business of rubbing up against human opinions, human feelings, human convictions and experiences, human anxieties and human needs, that he encounters at every turn the real meaning and significance of his faith in God.[5]

I do not believe that, at this time in the Church's life, the paid ministry should be doing all the pastoring in a congregation, running around trying to keep the flock happy (that is, attending worship and paying their dues, if that's happiness). I believe a pastor should be willing to spend time with the one lost sheep, the person with the problem or the sorrow, the one who is feeling the icy blast of doubt or facing some critical decision—and give that person as much time as he or she needs—rather than keeping the other 99 who should be mature Christians from defecting! This is a word for the 99: don't expect your minister to visit you for nothing more than a quick cup of tea and a homely chat every six months unless you want him to neglect the one and go after the 99, but, equally, don't be reticent to ask for your pastor when you feel lost.

The temptation to neglect the one sheep is great—the one will not bring in money and may never warm a pew—but it is in pastoring the lost ones that the preacher discovers practical meaning and significance in Christian faith. 'To love to preach is one thing,' wrote Richard Cecil (1748–1810); 'to love those to whom we preach, quite another.'[6] Of course, we will take every opportunity to know the 99 as well, though perhaps not in the same way as in more relaxed days past, because as we get to know the people to whom we preach, so we discover how to speak to them from God. I can think of few more heart-breaking ministries than that of the intinerant preacher who has no pastoral dimension to his message.

And what of lay preachers? It is very important that more than half the time they devote to their ministry should be spent in pastoral work—lay preaching is definitely not just an up-front job for Sundays. To neglect the pastoral dimension will result in lay preachers writing sermons around their own problems. In our pastoring, our ears will be open to hear what other people are facing in life so that we can understand where they are.

This is a very difficult task for a preacher anywhere. No longer is there such a thing as a typical churchgoer or a monochrome church; thank God for this variety, even though it means that a preacher is quite likely to face a congregation of manual workers, pen-pushers, unemployed people, teachers, home-makers, people who left school gladly at 14 years of age and university lecturers who've never been out of an educational environment since the age of 4! When a preacher gets to know his people in all their diversity, he discovers more of how to say what God gives him.

The preacher keeps in touch with global issues. Unless he is to have a limited perspective, the good preacher needs to develop a worldview which is sufficiently well informed to help him at least to begin to sort out some of the issues. For instance, keeping in touch with important world concerns and wanting his people to keep in touch too, he may raise the rôle of our nation in Third World development, or immigration, or nuclear power and weaponry, or apartheid, or freedom of belief, or the rich 'north' and the poor 'south', and many more. He should keep his ears open during news broadcasts and take the trouble to read the kind of newspaper which will help him understand global issues.

I suspect that a lot of what we preachers call 'keeping in touch with contemporary issues' is too simplistic. We are grateful for pressure groups set up to support the Christian point of view in moral issues, and yet we find so often that the stark presentation of issues such as abortion is often a good deal less stark when clothed in human flesh. We appreciate those who encourage Christian faith and mission, whose enthusiasm for Jesus puts new heart into us, and yet we often find that they make no concessions to doubt— and can a Christian really be said to believe unless he knows the reality of doubt? Keeping abreast of contemporary issues means also keeping an open mind and refusing to paint theology or morality by numbers: it is in being aware of the shaded areas where the colours blur into one another that the preacher will effectively speak to those who are wrestling with flesh and blood issues.

The preacher keeps in contact with the world Church. Just over 200 years ago, William Carey approached a meeting of his brother clergy about overseas mission and the chairman ordered him to 'Sit down, young man. When it pleases the Lord to convert the heathen, He will do it without your help or mine'[7]—similar sentiments to those of the oft-quoted General Assembly of the Church of Scotland in 1796: '...to spread abroad among barbarians and heathen natives the knowledge of the gospel seems to be highly preposterous, in so far as it anticipates, nay even reverses, the order of Nature.'[8] One wonders how they supposed the Gospel ever reached Britain in the first place!

Yet many preachers flee from world mission in much the same way today. Their theology is more likely to display a lack of confidence in the Gospel than a total confidence in irresistible grace, but often the real reasons are simpler: if this financially hard-pressed congregation stays away from church until the central heating can guarantee 20°C, how can the preacher persuade them to have any deep concern for the world church? They simply wouldn't understand why anyone in some remote part of the world might walk ten miles every Sunday to be with the people of Jesus in worship!

One of the key factors in the growth of any church today is involvement in world mission. My nine-year-old daughter goes to an ordinary state school and in her class nine nations are represented (counting the English and Welsh independently, of course). Issues affecting the world church are here, *now*—unless you accept that, you will simply be sidestepping reality. To take just one example: Christian/Muslim relations in Britain are cautious and seem to improve when there is mutual trust between individuals and communities. When our fellow Christians in West Africa hear of this, facing the steady Islamic advance south with all the pain this has brought, they do not understand why we behave as we do; they are not sufficiently aware of our part of the world Church—but are we aware of theirs? With all the resources of the voluntary mission agencies and Christian development bodies at our disposal, we have no excuse for being so ill-informed, so restricted in our vision and so unimaginative in our enthusiasm for the Church throughout the world. The societies can usually find ways of placing preachers overseas for short-term experience and of bringing Christians from overseas for similar placements. More financial sponsorship of this kind of interchange at local level (which means sabbatical breaks and funding) would inevitably deepen the growth of all God's people—congregations as well as preachers—by enlarging our horizons.

The preacher is helped by a good imagination. If you can have a mental picture of something, you're more likely to describe it vividly and clearly than if you haven't. Unfortunately, imagination cannot be taught, but you can train yourself to be observant and to pick up true images of life. Not long ago, I joined some friends handing out Christian leaflets in a city centre precinct during one of those late-night shopping times before Christmas; we were distributing simple publicity leaflets. That was the place to see just how secular our nation has become! One man was so laden with shopping that when I offered him a leaflet he said, 'No thanks. I haven't got any free hands.' O Lord, if only you'd given him more hands! The illustration is obvious—the better for being local and personal—and cries out for development.

Connected with imagination is the ability to distinguish a true illustration from a false one. I have heard of preachers comparing the number of practising Christians in Britain with the number of people who travel by train in the rush hour, and with the number of people who attend soccer matches: the faith lives, we are told, because numbers prove it. But when I dabbled in statistics they told me, 'figures can't lie but liars can figure'; there's no deceit here, but these are meaningless illustrations. The number of people going to work in the rush hour at Paddington Station or Kings Cross is totally irrelevant to the number of church worshippers because the motives are entirely different. And the number of people at soccer matches has nothing to do with church attendance figures because one is a hobby (however all-consuming) and the other is the way of eternal life. Imagination and clear thinking must be kept together.

PICTURES WORTH A THOUSAND WORDS

Illustrations can be divided up into types: we begin with simple figures of speech: colourful, vivid imagery. This develops into the analogy, a simple comparison, and, from there, into the more complex allegory. The parables of Jesus include analogies and allegories; you need to be aware of the nature of each parable you interpret, or you could eliminate the Cross in turning the parable of the Lost Son into a complete allegory of reconciliation. From these relatively short illustrations, you can add traditional tales and fables, historical and biographical allusions, quotations, anecdotes and personal reminiscences.

Much of this material may not be your own, indeed, it would be arrogant of you to assume that your own experience and imagination could supply you with the majority of your illustrations. Sangster comments on the self-centredness of some preachers: 'Talking overmuch about oneself is a fearful fault in a preacher, and it is hardly less heinous when he constantly talks about his own wife and children.'[9] So you should be taking illustrations from others, in humility, but you must make these things your own, or you will be mouthing meaningless words and will not make contact with people. At a more mundane level, Sangster recalls the story of a conference speaker whose personal anecdote evoked gales of laughter, somewhat to his surprise, until he discovered that the same anecdote had been told in the same terms by a previous speaker who had addressed the conference before the second speaker had arrived! Books of quotations and anecdotes can be a great help but need to be used sparingly.

Insights and topical illustrations may be filed or (because they usually depend on the right moment) merely turned over a few times in the mind, in the bath or the car or on a walk—wherever you do your mental gardening. Let's say you are doing some shopping on Maundy Thursday and you see something which strikes you as significant for Good Friday; think about it and, if you can, use it, but you will find that it will probably lose all its significance if you store it for another year.

Biblical illustrations can be gained from reference books, but the best source is a mind informed by regular reading of the Scriptures. And what of things like quotations and articles in books and magazines? Our brains are marvellous creations, but mine, at least, can't hold everything I feed into it, so I need to have some means of storing and recalling some illustrative material. It has been suggested that, as you read a book, you should make a note of quotations and ideas, and afterwards index them at the back of the book. I simply don't have the time to do that. My own method is to store quotations and significant references to longer items in a card-index arranged according to general subject-headings.

Little bits and pieces from the books and newspapers I read, or the plays I see, or the comments I hear, get scribbled down for later transfer to my card-index (though many of them get discarded before they get to the cards). More electronically-minded preachers my prefer to keep an illustration file on computer disc.

Eight Commandments

1. Illustrate when necessary, not just because you have an apt saying or idea available. Illustrations may often need to be provisional; that is, capable of being omitted during the delivery of the sermon.

2. Do not introduce an illustration. Sangster asks:

> Who has not heard a wearisome preacher ambling forward with phrases like these? 'I heard the other day of a story which I think might illustrate this point, and which I would now like to pass on to you. You may judge for yourself whether or not it does, indeed, illustrate what I want to say...' Bah! He is nearly as boring as Thackeray who, in some of his books, can hardly get a character on the way without explaining why he chose this character... and not that![10]

When you bring in an appropriate illustration you can see the congregation waking up; if you warn them it's coming, you will lose that effect, even with superb material.

3. Do not illustrate the obvious. If your point is quite clear, don't bring in an illustration; the only excuse for doing so would be to give the congregation a little break, but be careful not to distract them!

4. Do not labour the point of an illustration. If you do, you'll feel like someone who tells a joke at which no-one laughs!

5. Do not use illustrations as arguments. What you are trying to do is to illuminate a truth in order to make the truth more visible; your theological building-blocks will wobble and crash to the floor if you take your illustrations as arguments.

This is a regular feature of talks for children, and it takes careful thinking to avoid. I remember admiring the careful preparation of a preacher with a radio-controlled car in church. The effort he put into it was enormous, and the effect was good. But you could not equate controlling a toy car with God's guiding a human life. As it is, I can't remember the point the preacher actually made, and I don't think that was it, but it leads me to the sixth commandment.

6. *Do not upstage your teaching with your illustration.* It is very easy for congregations to latch on to an illustration rather than the point of the sermon. Most of us have been thanked after a service for something we didn't say and had no intention of saying: usually, it's because we've not explained an illustration properly and have allowed people to think that the illustration is the point. Then they go on to dream up their own development of our image and end up deriving some very odd teaching from it! Anything that steals attention from the proper subject is not an illustration but a deviation.

7. *Do not forget to explain the necessary facts.* Just as when you tell the story, make a note of the details: you might easily quote some person whose position in history illuminates the quotation you are repeating—if you fail to refer (however concisely) to that historical dimension, you simply introduce a distraction.

8. *Do not glorify yourself.* R W Dale once warned a young preacher: 'My lad, remember *our* temptation is not as a rule money.' He pointed at the open vestry door into the crowded Birmingham church; '*That* is our temptation.'[11] A slick way with sermon illustration is often the route to a congregation's heart: that may be God's grace, and it may be the devil's trap. The old proverb reminds us that candles give light, but they are always consumed in the process.

So, if we are to make effective preachers we must keep in touch with the people to whom we speak, and the world in which they live. In humility, we draw from human life those illustrations that enable the Word of the Lord to touch our people. Stuart Blanch wrote of the spirit of an evangelist, but it could so easily be the spirit of any preacher: 'not necessarily a person with a striking style; not always a person with great charismatic gifts, but one who makes it easier for others to believe in God.[12] When that is true, Portia Honeysuckle, look out!

NOTES

[1] Helmut Thielicke, *How Modern Should Theology Be?*, p 10.

[2] Phillips Brooks, *Lectures on Preaching, 1877* (Allinson: London, 1895), pp 5 and 28.

[3] W E Sangster, *The Craft of Sermon Illustration* (Epworth: London, 1946), chapter 1.

[4] J R W Stott, *I Believe in Preaching* (Hodder and Stoughton, London, 1982), p 236.

[5] Charles Smyth, *The Art of Preaching 747–1939* (SPCK: London, 1940), p 5.

[6] Richard Cecil, *Remains*, ed Josiah Pratt

[7] E Stock, *The History of the Church Missionary Society* (CMS: London, 1916).

[8] A Mayhew, *Christianity and the Government of India* (1929), p 28.

[9] W E Sangster, *op cit*, p 26.

[10] *Ibid*, p 96.

[11] W B Selbie, *The Life of Charles Silvester Horne* (London, 1920), quoted from David Edwards, *Christian England*, vol 3 (Collins Fount: Glasgow, 1984), p 266.

[12] Stuart Blanch in *David Watson, a Portrait by His Friends* ed E England (Highland: Crowborough, 1985), p 211.

Chapter 7

WORKING IT OUT:
Saturday Night at the Grinds'

'I'm going to bed, my dear; don't wake me when you come up. I'm getting a bit fed up with this preaching business—another Saturday night ruined! It had better be worth it in the morning!' With that, Mrs Grind, the lay preacher's wife, flopped upstairs in her dressing-gown with a mug of cocoa and a magazine, leaving Mr Grind in the dining room surrounded by bits of paper and books and—it has to be admitted—covered in confusion!

Ernest Grind had been out to support his local soccer team, which was playing at home that day, and they'd only managed a miserable draw. But his mind hadn't really been on the game because he was due to preach at 10.30 the following morning, and not a single hopeful idea had come into his head during the week before! As he ate his supper, he began to worry even more about what on earth he was going to say and, after he'd watched the news in a vain attempt to pick up some topical hint, he was in the dining room by half-past seven with his paper and books. There was a Bible, a one-volume commentary, an enormous concordance (he didn't understand Greek but he was fond of telling the congregation how many hundreds of times some word occurred in the New Testament!), a pile of scrap paper, a large exercise book and a ball-point pen. Two invisible items were missing: one was his failure to read the Bible consistently and daily (he was rather weak-willed about making the time), and the other was his failure to keep in touch with God in prayer. (Even a moment of prayer before he began his preparation would have made contact with God, but even more important would have been a proper prayer-relationship with his eternal Father.) These two invisible items are, in fact, the most important of all—without them, all the commentaries and concordances and papers and pens are not going to be very effective. The people will soon notice, and people do not listen to preachers who speak about God and his Word but display that they give up very little time to their relationship with him, however hard they try to cover it up.

THE JOYFUL TYRANNY

I'm not saying that as long as you pray and read your Bible, you will never find yourself in Mr Grind's perplexed posture on a Saturday night—those who are inclined to such pious pronouncements (and they *are* said) have a very limited experience of human nature and of the way God handles his servants. It is, therefore, dangerous to make generalisations, but Mr Grind's problem is that he's made a start on his sermon too late, with too little previous study, with too little biblical background and too little prayer. And when he's finished preparing his oration, it will be too late to reflect on it before he preaches it; having preached it, what ought to have been helpful revisions will be awful regrets! I am afraid that what will come across tomorrow will be half-informed homely advice (which could as easily have been gained from the more bigoted Sunday newspapers): badly ordered, confusing, aimless and ill-digested; the most effective results will be a despairing congregation and a disgruntled wife!

So rule number one in putting sermons together has to be: don't begin with pen and paper on Saturday night. Whether or not you are preaching to some plan, begin on Monday with your Bible and your prayers, your eyes, your ears, your heart and your brain.

Donald Coggan described that daunting feeling which often overcomes preachers as a 'tyranny'.

I refer not only to the fact that Sunday comes around with an inexorable regularity and makes demands which needs must be met. I refer also to the fact that we know that we must not offer to the Lord a second-rate offering: only the best we can produce will do. I think of the demands which this makes on a man's freshness and devotion and thinking and praying. A tyranny indeed! But a *joyful* tyranny—who would be without it who has been called and commissioned?[1]

What are the causes of this sense of tyranny? One is the simple human problem of motivation: with so many things for all of us to do in the week, we imagine there will be some time on Friday, always subtly concealing from ourselves the fact that on Friday and Saturday we have a bigger list of jobs to do than the one we drew up the previous Monday!

Another is the fear that we can say nothing that would be for our people the Word of the Lord; the task of preaching always fills a preacher with a sense of inadequacy, with a 'Why *me*? What have *I* to say?'

And there is a third tyranny in preaching, particularly to the preacher who has a proper fear and love of the Scriptures: it is the tyranny of not knowing where to begin and how to approach the glory of the love of God without dishonouring the Word himself. No doubt you have a favourite part of the Bible—we all like to deny it, but deep down, most of us have—and my particular love is the writings of Saint John. I am certainly not alone as a preacher in seeing a special connection between our ministry and what John writes in the Prologue of his Gospel about the eternal Word (John 1:1–18): a passage which is often read in Christmas worship. Knowing that it was to be read in church, for days before Christmas I knew that I had to speak from it. But the more I looked at it and read it, the more I was struck dumb by what I read and felt totally unable to say anything that would not simply detract from the splendour of it. In the end, I found myself considering the contrasts of the Christmas story (the Lord of lords laid in a manger, the King befriended by shepherds, and so on) and, strangely, the words of John's Prologue came out from the page at me. The preparation of that sermon had been a tyranny but, when, as I trust, *God* took control of it, a joyful tyranny. For, though the preparation of our sermons is often accompanied by a good deal of searching and struggling, at the end of it there is joy when just one person heeds that command: *Listen to the Word of the Lord!'*

Naturally, there is a Parkinson's law for sermon preparation as for any other task, and it would be quite easy to spend an entire week getting ready for next Sunday's sermons—but then they would be mere academic exercises of little use to anyone. Most of us, on the other hand, operate on the converse of the law, and it is a constant source of surprise to us that we get away with so little preparation, so late and so starved of prayer.

Subject

Mr Grind has first to find his text or theme. Sometimes he has to preach as part of a series of sermons, and he's provided with a text or a subject. That's much the easier way for someone who preaches regularly because he knows immediately where he is and—if he is unfamiliar with the particular congregation—has a point from which he can begin. But someone like Mr Grind, who preaches frequently but nothing like as often as his minister, gets bothered by pre-set texts because it means he probably has to do a lot of background study, and he can't hide behind his latest ideas.

There's a tendency among preachers to cling to something they've recently experienced and to build it into the next sermon, whether it is relevant or not: I regret that this fault is especially noticeable in those who preach infrequently. One lay preacher I knew told me, 'I always end up with the two great commandments...' Yes, *always*! It was his trade mark, but I fear it may have betrayed an inability to bring the Word of God to people from whatever text is there. If the text or subject has not been pre-selected, then the familiar search must take place, and no one can give any rules about this except to say what has already been said: do not give your own religious ramblings the label of preaching just because you stick a biblical text on the front end! As one who is deeply involved with your people, search for the truth to meet their deepest needs; as one who can stand back at a distance, search for the truth your people cannot see because they are so close; as one who longs to know more of God's love, search for the truth which speaks of that love.

Style

The preacher, having found his subject, needs to assess the style which may be appropriate: is it gentle or fierce? Is it teaching or evangelism? Is it urging or inspiring? It may well be that, towards the end of the preparation, some modifications will be needed to this initial evaluation, but at this stage it will give the sermon a basic feel. Clearly, this spirit needs to arise out of the bringing together of pastoral experience and the biblical word; it should not arise out of your own emotions unless you have at least checked those emotions with a trusted and wise colleague or friend, though sadly it often does. A vicar I know well had his beard regularly singed by the heat which was generated after his arrival in the parish: so his kind curate thought he'd make things better by roundly chastising the entire congregation one Sunday morning for the attitudes of a few! It was a kind gesture arising from emotions of anger and loyalty, but all it did was to worry the majority of the congregation who didn't know anything was amiss. Anger in particular can be both a powerful force and a dangerous trap for preachers: as in the case of John the Baptiser, and Jesus in the temple, it can be right and serve the cause of truth (Luke 3:7–20; Mark 10:14; 11:15–18), but it can sometimes be equally wrong (James 1:19–20).

Context

Having worked out the text and found its spirit matching the pastoral needs of the people, Mr Grind has to take a closer look at the context in which he will be preaching—he finds it helpful to close his eyes for a moment and imagine the scene in the church. Who will be there? What sort of congregation are they—are they, for the most part, well educated, or young, or elderly, or a bit distant or very friendly? What time of day is it (a pleasant summer's evening, a snowy winter's night, a cheerful family service with a lot of infants squawking, a formal service with little participation—boring the under 50s stiff—or a youth club special —building up a big head of steam in the over 50s)? Preachers learn a good deal of their craft from their congregations—few good preachers would deny that—and they also become quite astute at summing people up! It doesn't take long for a pastor to discover those who are geriatric in their twenties, the elderly who never grow old in spirit, and those folk with at least one foot on the brake pedal who are in between and beginning to feel their age! A sensitive preacher learns how to speak to everyone in such a way that they hear the Lord most clearly; that's why it often takes a couple of years for a preacher to begin to communicate effectively with his people.

Mr Grind is known to the congregation because they see him at the front most weeks, but his own personal friends (who happen to be people with grown-up families in the pre-retirement age range) are not representative of the needs and feelings of the *whole* local church. He is therefore at a distinct disadvantage in his preaching because his pastoral experience is partial—but be careful how you tell him, because he may not believe you! When he imagines the congregation, he doesn't always see what's really there—but nor do most of us.

Length

Having sorted out the context of the sermon, he will know what sort of length to aim for. I am one of those frightful preachers who rarely keeps to time, but I do try! At an early-morning service, I aim for 5 minutes or so; at our satellite congregations, where things are deliberately less formal, I aim for about 10 or 12 minutes; at a typical main morning or evening service, I aim for about 20 minutes or so. By 'aim' I mean, in fact, that I think that will be the minimum and that an overshoot of 25 to 50% is not unlikely with the wind of the Spirit in the right direction! Length needs to be partly instinctive. When more than one in ten falls asleep, it's much too long.

Associated with length is the way in which the preacher plans to put over his message. In order to stay as moderately sane as I can ever hope to be, I am not ashamed that I use the same sermon notes in two places on a Sunday. It is a lesson I was forced to learn in rural ministry: the sermon I preached at the 8 o'clock Communion is the same one I use at one of the mission churches at 9.30. The amount of written material averages about one-and-a-half cards and consists of bold headings with some detailed notes: at 8 o'clock, I more or less read it all out because it is the hearing that counts; in contrast, at 9.30, I simply glance at the headings to keep me on the right track (even though 9.30 is a bit early for my brain) because it is the contact of the whole personality that counts on that occasion.

Background

At this stage, the background reading comes in. If there's been a series of sermons on some subject, it may be that there's a useful book to read: some kind of commentary (not necessarily a biblical commentary) with which all preachers ought to familiarise themselves. Let's say you're taking a sustained look at John's Gospel. You should then be reading something like William Temple's *Readings in St John's Gospel*[2] over a period of time, in addition to a commentary on particular verses.

When it comes to the detailed Bible study, it is important to be able to find a good commentary that suits you—that is, one which you can use comfortably. If you're a lay preacher, you may begin with a one-volume edition and gradually build up a wider selection by taking advice from those who have been at it longer. A word of warning needs to be issued to any who like their commentaries to confirm their own opinions: do, please, remember that God has not called you to pronounce on your own opinions, however correct you may be sure they are. Popular devotional commentaries (the equivalent of this book) have their place, but you do need to train yourselves to read more widely and deeply. The first publication of Matthew Henry's *Exposition of the Old and New Testament*[3] is dated 1706, and it has enjoyed considerable popularity since then; however, it is astounding that some late twentieth-century preachers are still using this as the basic commentary to inform their preaching, as though it were itself holy writ! That is not to say one should not consult Matthew Henry or anyone else—I do quite often—but not as the main source of theological comment for today.

In using commentaries and reading around, make preliminary notes, some of which you will use in your final sermon-notes, some of which you will store in your mind, some of which you will discard. It's a good idea to write down concise quotations which you may want to use, but otherwise translate what you read into your own words when you make preliminary notes, and then to do the same again if you add them to your final notes, so that these thoughts become your own on the way. The notes you end up with are likely to be comments on various verses or words, important interpretations you may have missed and something from the wider context.

Your next task is to sort out from what may be quite a jumble of notes the important material for the sermon: the relevant textual comments, the issues and principles raised, the possible links and themes, and so on. At this stage, you don't need to consider structure too closely, simply to order the material you have gained from your reading. Now go back to the text and read it over clearly to see what comes out of it, or return to your basic theme, so that you can begin to see how some of what you have put down in note form has already worked its way into your thinking. At this stage, resist imposing your own ideas: continue to look out for God's leading. An aim may be developing in your mind, but do not yet commit yourself to it. It is a good idea to make a note of your thinking at this stage, and you will often find that a structure begins to appear.

What is the preacher looking for in his studying? Commentaries and learned books contain a mass of information on the subject of his sermon, so is there a sieve through which he can pass that information in order to leave behind what he wants? He is *not* looking for knowledge of the theories (these will simply help him to think straight): in biblical study, he is looking for:

1 the writer's intention
2 the meaning for today
3 the call of God.

Illustration

During this process, if your mind is alert (and that's another good reason for not leaving this until Saturday night), various ways of illustrating what is developing will either become apparent to you, or you will have to do some research to find something. This is where your wider reading and your observation of human nature and the world will pay off: a mind developed to see similar patterns of thinking in everyday, 'concrete' situations will find illustrating easier than one which can only follow a single thought-pattern. Despite what all the experts say (and I am aware of all the dangers), some of my illustrations come to me (I trust they are given to me) when I am preaching because of the response I perceive as I preach. You can sense whether a congregation is with you on some point, and if it is not, then retelling a story or freshly illustrating some point is vital. But helpful on-the-spot illustrations will come from familiarity with your background material: you must know what you're talking about, and that means you need a couple of days for your mind to turn it over.

One important aspect of your illustration is to know what is going to illuminate your theme and what is going to distract from it. I recall a splendid sermonic description of a walk around two-thirds of the walls of Jerusalem by someone who was very familiar with the city; it took up five minutes or so of the sermon, until the preacher reached the Pool of Siloam. It created a marvellous atmosphere, but it completely stole the show from the sermon, which must have been from John 9. What I gained from the sermon is what I could have gained from a photographic guide to the Holy Land; what I lost was the subject and the teaching. Illustrations must point to the theme clearly. Usually, that means reducing what you *can* say about something to what you *need* to say about it. We all love to tell people more than we need about whatever we are talking about—take the many historical equivalents of the sense of frustration felt by that great man of action, John, as he heard from prison of the slow progress of Jesus' ministry (Matthew 11:2–19). It would be an easy temptation to waste a lot of time in interesting but distracting biographies of 'Christians up against it' when such parallels ought to be concise in order to be effective. Do not let illustrations take over!

When relating stories, we have to tell them simply and entirely. Have you ever heard a child trying to retell a fairly complicated action joke from television? '...And so he jumped on his back and said to him; oh yes, and the man at the beginning was there on his bicycle, the one with the striped pullover—no, the man, not the bike—but before he said it to him, the woman—the girlfriend of the man with the wooden leg—came round the corner on the steamroller...' You remember the feeling? That's how some of our congregations feel when we tell them Bible stories or illustrations! Make sure you have all the relevant facts—no more—in the right order, and that you have a note of each one.

Failure to make a note of the details of a story can be fatal! A bishop discovered this after he attended a businessmen's lunch at which the speaker began by arresting his audience: 'I spent several years of my life in the arms of a woman who is not my wife: my mother!' This sounded just the story to wake up the back row at the diocesan conference on the following Saturday. He began, without notes: 'I spent several years of my life in the arms of a woman who is not my wife!' The audience's sudden intake of breath took him quite by surprise and eventually he broke the silence with, 'But I can't remember for the life of me who she was!'

Never read out a story verbatim: they only just get away with it on some children's television programmes (and that's often a near thing) but they have autocues to help them. When you're telling a tale, you must tell the congregation in your own words from one-word notes. Some may think it's wrong to embellish Bible stories a little, but as long as the original intention is clearly preserved, it can be helpful (and I know I'm on safe ground when I say that the stories of Jesus were summarised for us by the Gospel writers). Story notes come from this stage of preparation.

Extempore?

Earlier in the chapter the subject of extempore preaching was touched upon. Extempore preaching and 'a few words off the cuff' are poles apart. One comes from being gifted and skilful, the other comes from having kissed the Blarney Stone! Sermons which are to be delivered extempore or with very few notes have to be studied with the same care as those which are to be delivered with full notes—the difference is that in preaching extempore more of the thinking needs to be retained in the preacher's mind.

Extempore preaching will depend to a considerable extent on the response of the congregation at the time, so it is imperative that the preacher knows his way around all his material. As a student, I protested to the Scottish preacher James Stewart about my tutors' insistence that I should write out every word of my sermons, even if I later turned them into notes. He told me I should do so for at least ten years! Being an incorrigible rogue, I still prefer Simeon's older and rather quaint advice:

> I do not advise any young Minister to preach extempore until he has preached three or four hundred written sermons; until he has been at least three or four years' preaching. Let him speak, meanwhile, extempore, in his workhouse or schoolroom addresses, the same sermon which he has delivered in church from writing. He will thus acquire the habit of speaking easily and efficiently. After a few years, let him drop the fully written sermon for copious notes, and then gradually pass to extempore speaking. Carefully let him avoid anything like slovenly preparation. Let his extempore preaching be neither the result nor the cause of indolence.[4]

Certain elements in a sermon *must* be spoken directly to the people. Any kind of appeal must involve your eyes meeting theirs; stories must be told in your own words and manner; primary facts (the critical moments in Christ's life and their significance, for instance) must come straight from you, even when you are giving them a particular slant. If you can't do it any other way, then memorise it, though I would find that hard to do. Some people may find it helpful to practise with a cassette recorder. For me, these key extempore areas need one-word cues on paper and plenty of thought beforehand.

DIVIDE AND CONQUER!

Now comes the final pattern. There are many ways of dividing up a text or a subject—in fact, each one is different every time—but certain patterns can be noticed. There may be verbal connections: if your theme is 'Money', for example, you may use four subheadings each containing the word 'money' (and, if possible, similar phrases in each case); or you may find some alliteration, a form which is looked down on by current fashion but has an ancient pedigree. (I still benefit from a sermon I heard about 20 years ago on 'Advance, Adventure and Abandonment', a super picture of discipleship for a young Christian.) In addition to possible verbal connections, the pattern must be plain and easy to follow, whether or not it is apparent.

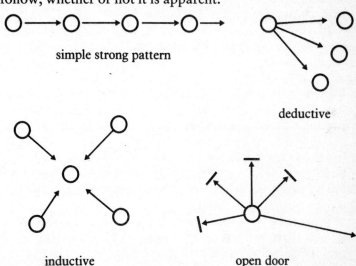

simple strong pattern

deductive

inductive   open door

There's the *simple story pattern* in which each idea proceeds from the previous one. But beware of this becoming a ramble! Alternatively the *inductive pattern*, with several different points of view looking in at the theme; or the *deductive pattern*, with several points derived from a central truth; or the *open door pattern*, in which we search various alternatives to find the truth.

Each pattern has its own way of applying the truth it brings to light. Finding the right pattern to fit the subject must, in the end, become instinctive—it should be one of the divine gifts most coveted by preachers. There are many more patterns than those illustrated, but the importance of pattern (or shape, or structure—call it what you will) is that being aware of it makes us aware of the silly additional shapes we sometimes add, like a fine Georgian house with a flat-roofed extension on the side or a beautiful brick ter-raced house with a mock Adam doorway! Sermons are most effective if they are memorable, but memorable illustrations and memorable structures are no use unless the heart of the sermon is even more memorable: that is what all our illus-trations and structures must serve.

Having developed the structure, we then fit into it what is necessary from the notes, ideas and illustrations we have been collecting. Of course, we will have far too much already, so we need now to relate what's there to the people we will be addressing. That should help us with the liberal use of blue pencil, striking out all the excess material—probably even some of the ideas we prized most!—and leav-ing us with a reasonable amount of the right type of material for the job. By now we may want to set ourselves an aim, and I guess that even those of us who rarely work out an aim have a pretty good idea where we are going. I was taught to write a short sentence aim (or was it 'goal'?) across the top of the front page of my notes; I've always been suspicious of it (and therefore have rarely done it) but I can appreciate that it concentrates the preacher's mind.

You're now nearing a full set of notes in the right order, and the beginning and ending must receive proper attention. The days have gone when chanting out a text and giving the reference will alert anyone to a sermon! A good beginning, with an arresting and clear introduction, makes a very important contribution. The varieties are infinite but let it suffice to say that the introduction should always be concise and should throw up the most important underlying idea or action of the sermon. Endings are similarly important (and even more difficult): they need not be summaries of the whole sermon—that sometimes reminds me of an aeroplane gradually slowing down and descending to land: It seems to take a long time and is a bit of a let-down. We may even introduce a contrast, as long as it is familiar, which will set the congregation thinking later, or there may be a challenge or a provocation, or an encouragement, or something devotional. Make it simple; make it short (because you mustn't read it out); leave the people wanting more.

If there is such a thing as a typical sermon, it needs to emerge from full notes (a full script in the early years) into pulpit notes. The detail on those notes will vary from preacher to preacher and from place to place. Tricky explanations need to be carefully written down and well understood—avoid extempore theologising about the doctrine of the Trinity, for instance! A full script may be the right form in a few places (I think of some cathedrals where the preacher is invisible to all except those with long sight or X-ray vision to see through pillars!): there the communication is verbal and aural.

But for most of us, truth is communicated from person to person, and that means the preacher must wean himself off taking a full text into the pulpit every time, no matter how good he is at reading it casually. Full texts, even those written in the best spoken style, go from the mouth to the ears and not often on to the brain, let alone the heart; people begin to look at their shoes: they can keep up their concentration for 10 or 12 minutes, and then they lose the theme! A prophet communicates the Word of the Lord not only by what he says, but by how he says it, and by the personal contact he makes with people as he speaks.

TO TYPE OR NOT TO TYPE

Finally, a note on materials. You must choose the thing that suits you best, but don't go flipping the pages of a spiral-bound notepad over the front of the pulpit stand as you plough through 20 pages of notes—people will stop timing you and start counting the pages! You may use a word-processor for your initial notes and even for the finished article (very handy if you're adept at moving text around, but I find I can scribble far more on a piece of paper than I can type onto a monitor). You may prefer typescript or handwritten text, but it is as well to stick with one method. I always use handwriting because it means I can prepare material away from home and I can even scribble something in at the last moment!

The paper you use will be your own choice: a notebook, the fashionable pocket-sized files, cards, or, in my case, record cards punched and used from one of these small files. Why do I prefer cards? I find that light card is easier to handle than paper and my six-inch by four-inch cards can be moved discreetly without sheaves of paper being shuffled around (watch a magician at work distracting your attention so that he can do the mechanics of his trick unnoticed and try to be as discreet with your sermon papers). I also prefer to use my cards horizontally (it suits the way I write and the lines on the cards), so my sermon-cards are punched at the bottom of the page, written on one side only and flipped down for the next page; my filed illustrations are also on cards, punched at the top of the page so that they can be interleaved with the sermon and save undue writing (they're also easier to abandon that way). You need to use the materials you find most convenient and easy to handle.

The rule is, again, careful homework and conscientious devotion, combined with clear and original thinking. Sermon preparation simply cannot be done as a matter of course week after week on Saturday evenings. Mr Grind, for your wife's sake, as well as for the congregation's, please take more care working it out.

NOTES

[1] Donald Coggan, *On Preaching* (SPCK: London, 1978), pp 3 and 4.

[2] Macmillan: London, 1945.

[3] The reference is to Matthew Henry, *Exposition of the Old and New Testament* (There are many editions, the standard being Robinson: London, 1839).

[4] A W Brown, *Recollections of the Conversation Parties of the Rev Charles Simeon* (1863), p 178.

Chapter 8

GETTING IT ACROSS:
The Problem with the Parson

The Reverend Septimus Snuffle is a sincere pastor: he's a man of deep conviction with a genuine concern for people. Yet his fairly short ministry in the commuter village of Nether-on-the-Verge has turned out to be quite different from the peaceful pastorate he had envisaged. By nature, Septimus was a quiet sort of man, always deeply hurt by controversy, but his predecessor's over-long ministry had left him with a difficult inheritance! Soon he was in conflict with the long-established local church power block in controversies about his long sermons, the new hymns and songs, and preaching that was getting uncomfortably close—all this was too much for them to bear!

People tended to undervalue our reverend friend and his message because it was obvious that he was not comfortable in the pulpit. His college had taught him to write out his sermons in full in order to develop a 'spoken English' style (when you read aloud the English you have written, you begin to realise how stiff it can sound to the ear), and to discipline his thinking. Unfortunately, he'd never been able to break free of this formal style, mainly because he had nightmares about drying up! This was an irrational fear—he proved that regularly in his school assemblies and in home groups and talks to the Men's Fraternal—but it was a real one. Sometimes, he tried to bring a little spontaneous material into his sermons, but he had never been trained to think on his feet and he'd become so used to his full texts that he invariably ran out of words: 'As I was saying when I mentioned... that... just... about... if... when,' followed by some silent fumbling with his papers (in themselves a work of origami), a red face and an embarrassed congregation! He was, therefore, convinced that he could never be free of his word-for-word script, whereas all he needed was the discipline to reduce his full text to full notes.

Because of this technique, most of the time he spent looking at the papers on the pulpit desk, just glancing up once a sentence to look at the people. On the occasions when his eyes actually met those of someone in the congregation, he noticed that they seemed to react in some way—a wry smile, an averted glance, a puzzled look. He was momentarily distracted, and it took him a few more disconnected 'ums' and 'ers' to find his place again! So he got in the habit of looking just above people's faces and never making eye contact if he could help it. Parson Snuffle feels slightly offended that many people look away from him when he's preaching; they don't mean to be rude but, quite unwittingly, they find that it's easier to concentrate on what he's saying with their eyes fixed on a hymn book or a floral display or that stone angel with a squint who holds up the roof above the choir.

His style comes across reasonably well on radio, even if it sounds just a little dated by today's hot-sell standards, and would work well in a lecture room. What he has to say is good stuff, without any doubt, but he's got problems getting it across to the people of God in a typical church: it sounds more theoretical and distant than it is. What lessons can be learned to help the parson with his problems?

CLARITY

The preacher must speak clearly. Few preachers in our churches have the Eliza Dolittle problem of a thick accent that needs to be diluted in order to be understood by the whole congregation: there may be just a few people who need help in this way, who may have forgotten that some members of the congregation are not locals! In those nations where Christianity has become part of the culture, however, many preachers have the opposite problem of acquiring an unnaturally posh accent. These ecclesiastical voices are a normal development from the days when the clergy were generally the best-educated group in our society, so the clerical voice was the voice of academic authority.

There is also a lot of mimicry involved: if some world-famous preacher has a particularly pronounced fancy accent, it won't be long before people training for ministry pick it up and begin the slide that will develop in their early years of ministry into something much admired by sermon-cassetteers but quite foreign to people outside the sacred portals of the Church. The funny voices of their preachers seem to be perfectly acceptable, even a distinct advantage, to some Christians today; those who are more discerning will be tempted to question whether the preacher's message is as phoney as his accent!

Mimicry is the mother of the Gothic drone, the nasal snarl, the Wesleyan whine, heavy-breathed sincerity, the breathless sprint, as well as the assured neo-Eton-and-Cambridge and the Oxford growl. If these things are to be avoided, how should we speak? Naturally, and if we have an accent, using it without shame. We do not all have to speak with 'Received Pronunciation', described by the *Oxford English Dictionary* as 'the pronunciation of that variety of British English widely considered to be the least regional, being originally that used by educated speakers in southern England', but we do well to take note of it (regardless of whether we speak it) as a neutral national standard, and to realise that pronunciation is continually changing. Those of us who spent the formative years of our youth near the birthplace of Received Pronunciation and William Shakespeare are stuck with it, of course!

Emphasis is just as important as pronunciation; indeed it is almost the same thing, and it tends to be seriously neglected by those who speak in public. Take a simple sentence like 'Jesus died for our sins'. To say '*Jesus* died for our sins' is to emphasise that the Saviour was the one who died. To say 'Jesus *died* for our sins' is to declare that redemption was by way of the death of the Saviour. To say 'Jesus died for *our* sins' is to make the meaning personal and, probably, to suggest that he didn't die for anyone else's! To say 'Jesus died for our *sins*' is to say that our sins are the reason why Jesus came to die. To say 'Jesus died *for* our sins' is to make nonsense of the sentence. I hear people who lead worship telling the congregation: 'We are here to offer *to* God our worship, that we may know the greatness *of* his love...' and I wonder what on earth they think they are saying! The worst offenders are usually the ones who are trying too hard to be sincere, but it becomes sheer gobbledegook. Emphasis matters in spoken language, and the cadence and emphases of spoken English depend on the sense: the beauty of our language lies in the irregularity of its rhythms.

One other aspect of speech needs to be noted, and that is the preacher's response to the context in which he is speaking. When I preach in my own church, which has a barely perceptible sound reinforcement system, I speak naturally with a voice that ought to carry to the back. If I were to preach in an enormous, echoing cathedral, I would have to rely on there being a good public address system that could take my voice to all the corners of the church without excessive resonance. Preaching in a small hall, I would speak as loudly as I needed to communicate clearly with everyone. Conducting an act of worship in the home of a housebound Christian who is almost stone deaf, I would shout so loud that the neighbours across the road would say 'Amen' to our prayers!

A bishop I knew had a light voice and people were always complaining that they couldn't hear him, but no one liked to tell him too directly—in those days, at least, it wasn't done—so they used to say, 'If I were a deaf man sitting in the back row, I might have had difficulty in hearing you today.' The good bishop had but one reply: 'If you were a deaf man you would be foolish to sit in the back row!' The sad fact is that many people who are hard of hearing do sit at the back and then wonder why they can't hear! Of course, preachers should not mutter, should not habitually shout, and should not gabble.

HOLDING THE CRICKET BAT

The preacher must take care with the style of his language. Language is a powerful and important means of communication, and it needs to be handled carefully. Holding up a cricket bat, Henry explains to Annie:

> This thing here which looks like a wooden club, is actually several pieces of a particular wood cunningly put together in a certain way so that the whole thing is sprung, like a dance floor. It's for hitting cricket balls with. If you get it right, the cricket ball will travel two hundred yards in four seconds, and all you've done is give it a knock... What we're trying to do is to write cricket bats, so that when we throw up an idea and give it a little knock, it might... travel. [He picks up the script of a badly-written play.] Now, what we've got here is a lump of wood roughly the same shape trying to be a cricket bat, and if you hit a ball with it, the ball will travel about ten feet and you will drop the bat and dance about shouting 'Ouch!' with your hands stuck into your armpits.[1]

Good spoken English is not pedantic or pompous but is simple and straightforward both in construction and in its use of words. Spoken English often breaks some of the normal rules of the written language and can look rather ugly on paper.

Many people are under the impression that English is a rigid language, but a language developed (and developing) from so many different influences could never be rigid. The so-called rules about never splitting an infinitive and never placing a preposition at the end of a sentence are artistic guides, not rigid laws. Because the only English we study is the written form, we easily overlook the fact that our language is used far more in its spoken form and often fail to notice how much more flexible the spoken language is. Peter

Levi's new translation of The Gospel of John (1985)[2] is a splendid example of the language we speak, with many apparently incomplete sentences, changes of tense, peculiar repetitions and the like: to read it in silence is strange; to hear it is a lively experience.

We tend to pick up much of our phraseology and jargon from the Bible—older preachers from the King James Version, younger ones from the Revised Standard Version or one of the contemporary translations. Each translation is quite distinctive. The King James Version is beautiful, its rough and earthy rhythms (not unlike today's) often ruined by misplaced veneration, though its sentence construction and vocabulary are quite different from our own. The Revised Standard Version is bound to bear the marks of its conception in 1937 (completed 1952), a kind of twentieth-century reproduction of seventeenth-century English, reaching its zenith in Isaiah 60:6, 'A multitude of camels shall cover you'. There is the beautiful, finely sculptured English of the New English Bible, the language spoken in the common rooms of the older universities (where they know the meaning of palanquin, vintager, bedizened and scion). Roman Catholics and Protestants alike have gained from the splendidly dynamic Jerusalem Bible but have been a little bothered by its use of 'Yahweh' and 'holocaust' and the like, and Protestants have found it difficult to handle some of the verse numberings in the Old Testament. Among contemporary translations, the Good News Bible (which developed the 'dynamic equivalent' principle of translation pioneered by J B Phillips) has reigned supreme for a decade and its style generally matches well with the dynamic English of preaching. In some evangelical circles it is fashionable to laud and magnify the New International Version, though I myself have yet to discover why. The language we use in preaching is affected by the translation with which we are most familiar.

As we illustrate our message, we often unconsciously use pictorial figures of speech. These brief illustrations scattered through our language can be immensely helpful. Try reading Dylan Thomas and see how descriptive half-a-dozen well chosen words can be. Sangster recalls hearing Dr J H Jowett speak of the mission of Saint Paul: 'I once saw the track of a bleeding hare across the snow: that was Paul's track across Europe.'[3] Pictorial language can sometimes be followed by concrete active nouns and verbs; we may speak of 'the springboard of faith,' and we can follow it up with words like dive, bounce, plunge, splash, immerse, drown, float, and so on. On the other hand, we must be careful with vivid metaphors, especially if they are inclined to come to us on the spur of the moment; in recent years I have heard a preacher quite inadvertently equate God with an engine, saying 'God is like that,' when God is not like that at all! This is a trap for those who have the gift of colourful expression and it needs to be carefully controlled—be particularly cautious about descriptions of God. Metaphors can sometimes be overdone, as in the classic speech of Sir James Sexton, MP, to a constituency meeting in Lancashire:

> Comrades, list to the clarion call! The plank of progress is now ripe for plucking. Soon shall we see the Socialist avalanche descending from the mountain tops and, with its mailed fist, crushing beneath its iron heel the capitalist snake in the grass which is barring the progress of the flood-gates of democracy from walking hand-in-hand with the British lion over the rich fields of prosperity from which we draw the sweet milk of iron, coal, and cotton.[4]

A WAY WITH WORDS

The preacher must be careful with words. Experts are very fond of technical language. An *Abergavenny Chronicle* of 1877 recorded a meeting of the British Association at which they were informed: '...in the meroblastic ova the biliminar blastoderm is discoid, but in the holoblastic vesicular.'[5] The observation of an aquatic experiment recorded that 'the biota experienced a 100% mortality response,' (which meant that all the fish died).

But it is not only scientists who play these tricks: you may have seen a low bridge described as an 'impaired vertical clearance' or a dustman described as a 'public hygiene (refuse disposal) operator', or you may have heard a preacher explain that 'without the incarnation of the eternal Word there could be no perfect and sufficient sacrifice, oblation and satisfaction for man's transgressions, nor true redemption and reconciliation'.

There are often good reasons for 'in' language, but not in preaching because the words a preacher uses are chosen for their inclusiveness, not to exclude the outsider. If you must —and sometimes you must—use words like 'incarnation', 'atonement', 'justification', 'reconciliation', and so on, never, never leave them unexplained. If you use them as shorthand in your notes, always remember to translate them each time you use them or, better still, find some way to avoid using them.

Verbal mannerisms can be very annoying to congregations, and yet the preacher is usually completely unaware of their existence: we soften statements with 'perhaps' and 'if you like'; or we close up gaps with 'you know', 'in effect', 'I'd like to suggest to you', 'there is a sense in which' and so on. Listen for a moment to the cultural jargon that flows freely at some prayer meetings, and hear the Lord asked if he 'might just' do so many things (I wickedly counted thirty-nine uses of 'just' in one fairly short prayer recently). I do not mean to say that all our praying should be in impeccable English—far from it—but, for those who can easily handle the language, the way we use words when we pray and when we preach may speak of an impoverished faith.

We need also to keep an ear on the way we put words together. It is said that a minister, in announcing that guest preachers would be present throughout Lent at Sunday evening services, concluded: 'If you wish to know who will be coming to preach, you will find them all hanging in the porch.' Bishop Douglas Feaver, a notorious dealer in words, is said to have hated after-church bun-fights (of which all church dignitaries have their fill) and, after ten minutes, was looking for his wife so that they could leave. In desperation, he boomed: 'Katharine, time for bed!'[6]

Less clever preachers can fall into some amusing traps, like the young pastor who constantly referred to conversion as 'the change of life', to the dismay of about half of the congregation, and those, including me, who have been known to speak of crossing our eyes and dotting our teas!

> 'Words don't deserve that kind of malarkey,' says Henry to Annie about using words in a prejudicial way. 'They're innocent, neutral, precise, standing for this, describing that, meaning the other, so if you look after them you can build bridges across incomprehension and chaos. But when they get their corners knocked off, they're no good any more... I don't think writers are sacred, but words are. They deserve respect. If you get the right ones in the right order, you can nudge the world a little or make a poem which children will speak for you when you're dead.[7]

BODY TALK

The preacher uses his body as well as his words. It is often appropriate for a preacher to use natural gestures to underline the meaning of his message; he may point to a cross in the church in speaking of the centrality of the death and resurrection of Christ; he may describe two imaginary parcels in order to demonstrate some paradox; he may raise his arms in prayer or praise; he may depict God's grace with a heaven-to-earth movement—and these body-figures can be very important. However, some of us are inclined to use our arms like windmills and to fidget with our feet, and we need to be restrained because these can so easily distract from what we are saying. An audience that is fascinated or irritated by our antics will not hear clearly what we have to say, so we need a bad habit corrector (unless we have a spouse, who will naturally do the job without being asked). When we talk with another person, we often use our hands to create the shapes and senses of what we are saying, though these gestures are usually meaningless to others. That doesn't seem to matter in conversation, yet it becomes annoying in preachers. By all means, let us use gestures freely, but always descriptively. Bishop Hensley Henson, a great preacher and a man held in some awe by lesser men, is said to have had a magnetic gesture in which he would slowly swing out his arm in a huge arc and then touch his lips with his index finger before a torrent of powerful words burst forth. One inquisitive (and fearful) student dared to ask him the origin of that intriguing movement (imagining that it might be the equivalent of Isaiah 6:7 or Jeremiah 1:9) and was told, quite simply, that he would discover for himself when he had false teeth!

There is also a tendency among preachers to fiddle with things while preaching. I have found myself fiddling with the rim of the pulpit and the edge of the pulpit-stand or playing with my wedding ring, and if I had spectacles, no doubt I would play with them as well. A student friend of mine let out a little yelp at the beginning of a sermon in a North-country mining village and seemed so worried that he delivered the rest of his sermon without reference to his notes; when asked afterwards what was the matter, he explained that he had touched the brass pulpit-stand (on which there was one of those awful strip-lights) and was, in his words, 'connected to the national grid'!

The way we use the language of our bodies in worship is important, particularly in those traditions where posture is used to strengthen meaning. We try hard to remember that we are engaged in humanity's highest activity, even when we have to hold back laughter as we announce that the Ladies' Circle is having a lingerie party next Tuesday, or when someone prays for newlyweds 'that they may have wisdom in the conduct of all their affairs'! That does not mean we adopt the posture of some marble effigy in the pulpit, but it does mean that all of the offering of our worship and our lives and our preaching is the best.

N.B.

The preacher must use his notes properly. The *Oxford English* guide to the language informs the after-dinner speaker that he must not read his notes: 'A speaker who is nose-deep in notes is wearing self-imposed blinkers: he cannot communicate effectively.'[8] Let your notes restrain you from getting so carried away that you preach a sermon about a miracle of two loaves and five fishes—I wonder how many times that has been done?—or that what you end up saying badly is very different from what you had prepared carefully. Make sure your notes are accurate—look up facts rather than generalise—and know when it's best to read out part of your notes verbatim.

Bishop Harry Moore, General Secretary of the Church Missionary Society, was drawing its 1986 General Council to a close with a most stirring sermon against the luncheon-bell; realising the time, he read a couple of sentences of his notes, and, though they made sense, it was obvious that they needed unpacking, so he picked up the papers and peered at them with the words, 'Who writes these scripts anyway?' If you can manage without your notes and without drifting off into some other theme, all well and good; and if you can see that the point you have just made has not been understood, be ready to go back again briefly for a fresh attempt. The KISS rule developed over many years by clergy families still applies: Keep It Simple, Stupid!

When using notes, be sure that you understand what you've written! It seems silly to say, but it's a common mistake. The only way to be sure is to make an unalterable rule of going through the entire sermon beforehand (perhaps the day before) as though you were preaching it. If you leave a few spaces, you can add in a word or two or, more likely, cross something out.

Some preachers never keep their notes. Others, like me, have kept them all. Those who throw them away could be accused of wasting a possible resource, and those who keep them could be accused of arrogance. My own reasons for keeping my notes are that I sometimes turn back to look at how I have tackled a text or subject in the past—by 'sometimes' I suppose I mean about once every couple of months. The biblical material is, as you may expect, less subject to decay over the years, but the illustration and the application changes considerably with the passage of time. Nevertheless, I am not afraid to admit to times when I can't see the way forward and need to look up one of the indices (of texts and subjects) of my sermon filing-system to see if the past can help me. It may be that I simply need to refresh my mind on some textual point, or I need to find a suitable thought pattern, or I may need a way in to the subject. On rare occasions, I may re-use an entire sermon from the past, though only for the simpler type of sermon, or for one that is more purely exegesis, normally after writing it out again.

EYEBALL TO EYEBALL

The preacher must speak to his people's eyes. 'I must be able to look my people in the eye... for preaching is an essay in co-operation,' wrote Donald Coggan.[9] When I was in training, one of my teachers told me that if anyone turns down the lights as you begin preaching, don't go on until they have all been turned back on again. The preacher is not an actor on a stage: he is relating to people, and he must be able to see the people and to respond to them, even if, like Parson Snuffle, he finds it a little hard to cope with the reactions on their faces! The sermon is not the time to save on electricity; a much more economical and sensible way to do that is for all the congregaton to sit near the front so that the lights can be turned off at the back. The preacher must always look at the people when he is addressing them as individuals, and in looking he must love them. Simeon told his students:

> *Let your preaching come from the heart*—love should be the spring of all actions, and especially of a Minister's. If a man's heart be full of love, he will rarely offend. He may have severe things to say, but he will say them in love. People will soon see whether a Minister is speaking in his own spirit, or merely declaring God's message.[10]

Relating to people is what preaching is all about, bringing the preacher and his people into such a relationship with one another that together they may come into a relationship with God himself. Preaching is personal, which is why people who don't want a personal religion generally find good preaching disturbing, and it is personal because our faith is in the personal and living God who is our Father.

In preaching personally, to the eyes, the preacher who is rightly fearful of the word must also be fearless of the truth. If he is sufficiently convinced of the truth that he takes his people to task, he must also be prepared to take the full consequences. That could easily mean prolonged unpopularity, a period of difficult relationships, and the temptation to run away. Remember that in 1782, Charles Simeon was first locked out of his church, his people were then locked out of their pews; but he stayed there for 54 years! As long as the preacher with a severe message to deliver knows that he speaks to people just like himself; as long as he is convinced that what he says comes from God, and as long as he loves the people, he should be able to endure. It's all very subjective, I know, but what more can be said?

Never apologise beforehand for the feebleness of your words, unless you wish to waste your time and effort. 'Speakers who begin with apologies for inadequacies they have not yet had time to prove,' advises the *Oxford English* guide, 'have a kind of death-wish, yet this self-debasement is common.'[11] It is a miracle often repeated that the Spirit speaks to people most clearly when the preacher is least satisfied with his work.

JOINED AT THE NECK

The preacher must not neglect the emotions. Martyn Lloyd-Jones described preaching as 'theology coming from a man who is on fire.'[12] No doubt the argument between head and heart in the Church will go on until the end of time, but is it based on anything more than prejudice? Those who want it all warm and secure despise what they see as the coldness of some preaching—the apparent lack of joy and zest in faith —while those who want it all neat and tidy despise what they see as the abandonment of reason, the loosening of all doctrinal restraint. When will these people realise that we all have necks? The human neck is a very important part of the anatomy, for it joins the head with the heart. Any preacher who so stresses the one without the other bears a striking resemblance to one of the victims of Madame Guillotine! We must neither neglect, nor become the plaything of our divinely implanted emotions: let us be willing to laugh and to cry as we bring the Word of the Lord to real people. Luther once said,

> A bee is a small animal which makes sweet honey, but which nevertheless can sting. So the preacher has the sweetest consolations, yet when roused to anger he can say biting and stinging things.[13]

PREACHER, PREACH TO THYSELF!

None of us succeeds in having entirely pure motives, but it must still be our first aim, for without it, our preaching is a hollow sham. This is a two-sided matter. The first is quite simple: being one person in the pulpit and another when out of it is no way to preach. 'O for a forty parson-power to chant thy praise, hypocrisy!'[14] But what of the second—the preacher who has real problems yet is unwilling to admit to them among his people? C S Lewis, in *The Sermon and the Lunch*, wrote of a cleric whose teaching on family life differed from his practice:

> What worries me is that the Vicar is not telling us all that home life is difficult and has, like every other form of life, its own proper temptations and corruptions... The trouble is not that he is insincere but that he is a fool. He is not talking from his own experience [of family life] at all: he is automatically reproducing a sentimental tradition—and it happens to be a false tradition. That is why the congregation have stopped listening to him.[15]

A preacher who is willing for his ministry and message to be tested in the fires of pastoral ministry at its hottest will not retain his integrity if he defends himself with a wall of piety or beyond-reproachfulness.

> There is a sense in which every minister of the gospel is diminished by his ministry. If he has any self-knowledge at all, his ministry makes him less confident in himself, less assured, less doctrinaire and therefore sometimes less secure. He becomes more aware of the dark places in his own life and in the lives of others.[16]

The necessity for a consistent lifestyle does not only mean that he seeks God's grace, like any other Christian, to lead a holy life, but that the whole of his life bears the stamp of reality and integrity on it. Too many pastors, priests and lay preachers hide behind their office and status because they are frightened that people outside the close circle of their friends will discover some of the emptiness inside. The preacher must seek to be what he preaches and to preach what he is in the grace of God. 'If any man will live as faithfully as he preaches,' wrote Simeon, 'he will lose his popularity with the upper classes, and will get no Bishopric.'[17] We must never call people to perform tasks which we are not willing to share in ourselves—especially the humble and dirty and thankless tasks—nor call them to give their efforts and then fail to give our own. The preacher who urges his people to go to home groups and is known to stay at home when there's a good match on television, or who won't turn out from his home on more than three nights a week, must either be ready to change his ways or to stop preaching in that way. If what is said in the pulpit is not in some way a reality in the preacher, his sermons are worse than wasted. He may stand several feet above the people of God in the pulpit, but in their ministry and mission he must stand with them.

> The attitude you should have is the one Christ Jesus had:
> He always had the nature of God,
> but he did not think that by force he should try to remain equal with God.
> Instead of this, of his own free will he gave up all he had, and took the nature of a servant.
> He became like man and appeared in human likeness.
> He was humble and walked the path of obedience
>   all the way to death—his death on the cross.
>
>   (Philippians 2:5–8)

The word 'servant' is a frequent description of God's messengers in the Bible; a word used supremely of God's missionary Son; a word which must describe the preacher. It is not an easy title to accept, and one that can sometimes cause more pain to the families of the servants than to the servants themselves.

Finally, the preacher must realise that God is the Lord of preaching. Despite all that has been said about technique in getting the message across, every Christian preacher, lay and ordained, knows that God is in control of the message and must be in control of the messenger.

> Servant of God, I am bitter and desolate,
> What do I care for perfection of phrase?
> Cursed by your humour, your poise, your diction,
> See how my soul turns to ashes within me.
> You who have vowed to declare your Redeemer,
> Give me the words that would save.[18]

NOTES

[1] T Stoppard, *The Real Thing* (Faber and Faber: London, 1982), Act 2, Scene 5, p 52.

[2] Reference is to Peter Levi, *The Holy Gospel of John* (Churchman: Worthing, 1985)

[3] W E Sangster, *The Craft of Sermon Illustration* (Epworth: London, 1946), p 14.

[4] *Sir James Sexton: Agitator*, p 172, quoted from Sangster *ibid*, p 86.

[5] *The Abergavenny Chronicle*, 25 August 1877.

[6] John Kelly, ed *Purple Feaver* (Westgate: Northampton, 1985), p 15.

[7] T Stoppard, *op cit*, Act 2, Scene 5, p 54.

[8] I C B Dear, ed *Oxford English* (Oxford University: 1986), p 286.

[9] Donald Coggan, *On Preaching* (SPCK: London, 1978), p 50.

[10] A W Brown, *Recollections of the Conversation Parties of the Rev Charles Simeon* (1863), p 188.

[11] I C B Dear, ed *op cit*, p 287.

[12] M Lloyd-Jones, *Preaching and Preachers* (Hodder and Stoughton: London, 1971), p 97.

[13] P Smith and H P Gallinger, tr and ed *Conversations with Luther* (Pilgrim: Boston, 1915), p 196.

[14] F Page, ed *Byron Poetical Works* (Oxford: 1970) *Don Juan*.

[15] C S Lewis, *First and Second Things*, ed W Hooper (Collins Fount: Great Britain, 1985), p 57.

[16] Stuart Blanch in *David Watson, a Portrait by His Friends* ed E England (Highland: Crowborough, 1985), p 211.

[17] Quoted from H E Hopkins, *Charles Simeon of Cambridge* (Hodder and Stoughton: London, 1977), p 201.

[18] Quoted from I D Bunting, *Preaching at Communion (i)* (Grove: Nottingham, 1981), p 12.

Chapter 9

TALKING IT OVER:
Let's Have a Home Group!

It didn't take long for the message to get around that the new parson was a little different from his predecessor, and gradually the folk on the fringes of the church came to take a look. One of those was Mrs Elizabeth Sanctity. Mrs Sanctity—Liz to most people—is a young mother with a strong Christian faith, married to a man with not a lot of faith, and what faith he has seems to decrease every time his wife gets some more! Liz will do anything for anyone without a hint of a grudge, and her faith is lively and enthusiastic.

Well, it wasn't long before Liz had realized that Septimus Snuffle was a clergyman of firm conviction, and, from that moment, she was back in church and became his lively supporter in everything. Our vicar friend and his family are immensely grateful for the support Liz Sanctity gives to them: her help and encouragement during the rough passage of his early ministry in the parish have been invaluable, and her commitment to Christ (though often attacked by doubt and by the failure of her husband to believe) is a kind of proof to the preacher that the Lord lives and reigns. She loves to call in at the parsonage and discuss things she's read in the Bible or heard in church that have given her an important idea.

The biggest problem Liz has is caused by her greatest gift: enthusiasm. Her zeal for Christ and her longing to serve is too often isolated from a commitment to the existing patterns of church life. Now that poses no problems for the 'newcomers' in the village (newcomers are defined by the natives as people who've moved in less than 20 years ago). But those who've never dreamed of not going to church—

the ones who are deeply stuck into a style of religion from which they do not like to be dislodged—do not take so kindly to Liz! To be fair to them, they are the children who have never rebelled very much—the brothers of the lost son (Luke 15:25–32)—and, like most of us who are too unaware of it to admit it, they have rather assumed that the inheritance is theirs, and theirs alone! Their difficulty with Liz is that her energetic faith doesn't match their expectations; she obviously finds their rather starchy worship quite a struggle and is still occasionally missing on Sundays.

Even Parson Snuffle didn't find her easy to understand at first. Apart from his dislike of being nicknamed 'Septic', he found some of her opinions rather immature. Quite rightly, she realises that God's dealings with humanity are always personal, but she usually takes that to mean that God deals with us only as individuals; she is properly keen on Christian fellowship, but only with those she admires or views as possible converts; she is anxious that people should pray, but tends to reckon the value of prayer by the sincerity of the pray-er and how often he prays; she takes an active interest in the parson's sermons (and looks up all the references in her Bible), but she often complains to him that they are too informative, too cold and too far from the heart. Liz is an enthusiastic enigma.

But the thing that really got up the noses of the locals was when Liz stood up at the Annual Church Meeting and suggested: 'Let's have a home group!' Anyone would have thought she had uttered a very rude word! You simply don't say things like that at an Annual Meeting: you can take the pastor to task for his failures (in the nicest possible way); you can imply that the treasurer has cooked the books, and you can suggest a general appeal to rebuild the churchyard wall, but you don't suggest things like house groups. However, the newcomers instantly thought it was a good idea—after all, there had been home groups in most of the churches from which they'd come—and the locals were so taken aback that they were dumbstruck! The vicar didn't wait for the inevitable backlash, so a home group was set up, and the congregations of the other Christian churches in the area were invited to join in.

Preaching in today's Church usually goes hand-in-hand with groups for discussion and prayer. Most of these groups begin when someone like Liz takes a lead: someone with a lot of enthusiasm and deep Christian conviction, usually combined with some black-and-white opinions! Home-based groups are undoubtedly an important step forward in the life of the Church in this generation: indeed, it's rather odd that it should be necessary to say so in an age when so much good has already been gained from these gatherings. A church without at least one home group for Bible study and prayer is, thankfully, exceptional, though there are many churches where they are still viewed with grave suspicion! How do informal groups fit into a pattern where preaching is given a high priority?

THE VALUE OF HOME GROUPS

Home groups are the most important occasions for discussing the Bible in the context of our life's experiences. No matter how gifted the preacher, he cannot bring all your questions to the Bible, for each one of us comes with his own set of questions—and so a study group can be helpful in sharing these questions in the light of the Bible.

Home groups can also be helpful in inter-church relationships. Sadly, so many of us worship in isolation from one another on Sunday, each tradition observing its own eccentricities in clear separation from the others—small wonder the world fails to believe (John 17:21). But an ecumenical group can break down many of these false divisions.

Home groups can make Christian fellowship easier. In the larger churches, many people only come and go on Sundays. (Even with a building that makes Christian fellowship easy, there will always be many who find personal contact with anything more than a small group an overpowering experience.) They may have contact every so often with a minister, but they need a fellowship that's scaled down to a reasonable size: a group in which they can get to know others and be known.

In all these and other ways, home-based groups are meeting important needs and are also developing into significant units of pastoral care and of evangelism. They eat up a good pastor's time in many ways, but they are well worth that time. What happens in church on Sundays—the most important Christian event of the week—is certainly in no kind of rivalry with home groups. Those who have become familiar with church home groups know that the ministry of the monologue sermon is not killed off by discussion—quite the reverse. In fact, group discussion increases people's interest in and knowledge of the Bible and results in a greater interest in preaching. Nor can preaching afford to stand aloof from home groups, for these discussions can help to bring people to the Bible and are another way of alerting the preacher to the real problems faced by his people.

The best home Bible studies are the ones in which the teaching of the Bible is firmly planted in experience: those that try to ape sermons are not only unnecessary but are also doing the wrong job. If you want to kill off a home group from the best of motives, all you have to do is to think of it as a discussion-sermon. In addition to the discussion aspects of home groups, they also provide superb opportunities to convert Bible study into practical and informal prayer.

Apart from the now familiar pattern of home groups, the preacher can benefit from having a specific group to reflect on his preaching. This may be a particular group of people chosen by the preacher to help him to communicate and to make sure that he keeps in touch with contemporary issues, or it may be a normal church home group following up Sunday sermons with discussion. With no restrictions on a church's resources, it would be grand to have both types of group functioning, but we have to admit that, in most places, a special preacher's group is something of a luxury and possibly a clique. However, it should be possible, perhaps using an established home group, for preachers to receive some well considered feedback from their sermons: not the kind of idolatry that trips so kindly off some people's lips but is almost useless as a standard, nor the equally useless grudging ingratitude of those who always find fault. The preacher needs a way of drawing on honest and positive criticism from those who can help him in a variety of ways— with his thinking, his reflection, his emotions, the effect of his preaching, in practical ways of technique, and so on. Honest Christian criticism, given lovingly and received positively, is one of the finest tributes anyone (and especially any group of people) can pay to their preacher.

'The expertise of the pulpit can only be learned slowly and, it may well be, with a strange mixture of pain and joy,'[1] wrote Donald Coggan. Learning from the listeners can be a painful experience for any public speaker. They will want to comment on the content of his message, what he said and whether it can be defended: is the biblical message true to the whole of God's self-revelation, and are his reflections on the human predicament true to life? They may well suggest that he watch some programme on television, or go to see a film or read some important new book in order to fill in a gap in his perception of the world. They may want to hold him back a little, to make him willing to share people's doubts and to give him the kind of warning Albert Schweitzer (1875–1965) gave to preachers: 'When you preach the gospel, beware of preaching it as the religion which explains everything.'[2] Those who have been trained to assemble ideas may be able to suggest some help with the construction of his sermons, and those with a keen eye may be able to comment on how they are delivered. More important than any of these will be the group's thinking on the *effect* of his sermons: why did the one on death strike home when the one on Nehemiah didn't? What was the point of the sermon on Romans 1:16–17? What, if anything, were we left with from the sermon on Psalm 103? John Stott strongly encourages preachers to accept the criticism of a group of wise friends: 'lay critics,' as he calls them.

> When I began to preach at the end of 1945, I requested two medical students to act as mine... Although I remember being devastated by some of the letters they wrote me, their criticisms were always salutary... A preacher who belongs to a team ministry should certainly ask his colleagues for their comments.[3]

Francis Kilvert described a nineteenth-century clerical colleague who 'drew water out of rock like Moses and hit the people harder than Moses hit the rock.'[4] No doubt a little assistance from his congregation might have been useful, though probably unwelcome! And the most important question a group can prompt their preacher to answer is: 'Am I preaching Christ?' It can help him to take his task more seriously and himself less seriously.

In recent years many churches have acquired sound amplification systems which can be used not only to assist the hard of hearing but also to record cassettes of sermons. Even churches without sound systems can easily record sermons with an inexpensive cassette recorder and microphone. However, I don't think I'm alone in having some hesitations about this practice. In general, my own view is that there are four uses for recorded sermons: one is for the benefit of Christians who are housebound (how I detest the words 'shut in'); for them, extracts of a service and the sermon from their own local Christian family can be a source of strength. The second is for the benefit of those who have gained something special from a particular sermon and want to hear it again. The third is for those who have come from the church family and are now at a distance, such as friends, family, or mission-partners overseas—for whom extracts of special services and sermons can be a treasured link. The fourth is as the opener or the background for a discussion group. Thus sermons can reach out for a short period beyond the single occasions on which they were preached. Very few sermons last longer.

Some of the greatest sermons of all time are now not a great deal more than printed words in a book—interesting information, no doubt, especially to those with a taste for it, but not the same thing as the living Word. If you were to listen to recordings of radio or television comedy programmes from 20 years ago, with all but a few you would wonder what you used to find so funny! Humour rarely endures for long and I'm quite certain that the same is true of almost every sermon we preach. Just think how much money might be released for better purposes if 90% of the cassettes in church tape libraries were wiped clean!

SUPPORT GROUPS

Not so very long ago, preachers used to talk together about their craft but, in most places during the last decade or so, the practice has declined to extinction. We now have ministers' fraternals when we moan about our problems; we have meetings of clergy when we take occasional pot-shots at each other and never tell the truth about our failures; we have in-service training for pastors when we are told what to do by sociologists and academic theologians; we have much-needed preachers' prayer groups but we rarely get together as local groups of preachers, ordained and lay, to discuss and study the art of preaching. Professional ministers badly need this opportunity to reflect and study, and lay preachers need it even more—and they need to do this together. Why don't you try to set up a group? May I offer you a few questions to get you going?

1   You have decided on a 13-week series of sermons to introduce your people to the first half of the Gospel of John (chapters 1–11). How would you plan it and why?

2   The mayor and council are coming to your church this year for their annual service and, since you are mayor's chaplain, you are to preach. You wish to reflect on something of local significance—a genuine concern of the

community—and you also wish to speak something of the Good News in Christ. Where would you begin? What would your text be? And what would your sermon outline look like?

3 You are an assistant pastor and your boss has just been overcome with heat on the Day of Pentecost. Someone has just read Acts 2:1–12 and you have a four-minute hymn in which to prepare your sermon. Try it!

4 What significant book or play or newspaper article or television programme have you taken in lately? How has it affected you?

5 Choose a biblical book to read through in large gulps and then study it from a preacher's point of view.

The group serves as a complement to drinking at the well of prayer, for one of the problems all preachers face is how to find this space for special times of reflection. Part of the answer has been known to Christians and Jews for millenia, 'the daily office', an occasion of Bible reading and prayer, in some kind of liturgical framework which transcends spiritual moods, open to anyone to attend, disciplined by a set time, and a real meeting with God, regardless of whether anyone else attends. Preachers who may wish to reject that kind of discipline as too formal, or who allow themselves to slip out of this daily discipline because 'no one else will be there' do not know what they are missing. The making of space for God in our lives can appear to be a very mundane task!

That's why a support group can be helpful, especially for a preacher who has to work in an isolated or depressing ministry. This support can come from preaching colleagues, as I've suggested earlier, but this is often not as easy as it sounds for lay preachers and busy clergy, or it can come from godly souls who love the Lord in down-to-earth humility; either way, the support is vital. In my own parish, there are a few Christians who turn up for our daily prayers once or more during the week and then drop in to the parish office to make coffee or operate the photocopier or fold the pews-news or clean the silver; they under-estimate their value to those of us who preach. As we read the Bible together in our morning prayers, we come across bits that make us laugh or cry, bits that puzzle us and illuminate us, and we feel free to stop and reflect. Then we worship and pray, and move on to the day's work. Though there may appear to be no connection between the times we spend praying together and the times we spend working together, it is that prayer which gives meaning to the fellowship: it is communion in the Spirit. And for us preachers, the reading, the reflecting and the praying, combined with the passionate coaxing of a stubborn duplicator and the hurried drinking of a cool cup of coffee are the stuff from which good sermons are made.

A good preacher knows the importance of discussion in complementing the work of the pulpit; how helpful it can be for people to discuss what they have heard in a sermon; and how invaluable it is for the preacher to talk over his sermons with other Christians—people with whom there is complete trust and love. But there is one whose love is deeper than that of any Christian: our heavenly Father, who longs for those of us who preach to talk over our sermons with him.

NOTES

[1] Donald Coggan, *Convictions* (Hodder and Stoughton: London, 1975), p 163.
[2] Schweitzer, quoted by G F Seaver in *Albert Schweitzer, Christian Revolutionary* (Black, 1955).
[3] See J R W Stott, *I Believe in Preaching* (Hodder and Stoughton: London, 1982), p 272.
[4] Kilvert, quoted by W Plomer, ed, *Kilvert's Diary* (Cape: London, 1938), 3 vols.

Chapter 10

THE PREACHING PEOPLE:
Harnessing Jimmy's Energy

Jimmy Keen is the youngest member of Saint Guthlac's Church Council, but that isn't so special because you can be quite old and still be among its younger members! Jimmy is a recently trained teacher, and he comes from a completely non-Christian background: his parents didn't have him 'done' as a child, and they didn't even bother to pack him off to Sunday School. When he was at college reading athletics, studying the girls and smoking pot, he got mixed up with some Christians and found himself giving his life to Christ. In some ways he was a very unwilling convert, but undoubtedly a completely committed disciple. That is Jimmy's strength, and a very important strength it is. Jimmy knows what it's like to be a complete rebel, and he knows what it's like to meet Christ face to face in a dramatic encounter.

The Church today desperately needs more people with Jimmy's commitment and single-minded dedication to Jesus when very few trust in the Lord. He knows the way many people outside the Christian family feel about 'religion'—he knows that Christ has an irresistible attraction for them, yet they totally disdain the Church. The problem Jimmy has in communicating this message to his fellow councillors is that they simply don't believe him! In fact, most people in the Church today, despite what they say, do not really believe that the so-called 'Christian' nations are anything but Christian at heart. They acknowledge the fact that Britain (like many other developed nations) has had gigantic Christian influences on its past history, but that these forces are no longer at work in our society, yet they are unwilling to *believe* what they say.

Jimmy has tried to get his message across to the church council by telling them the famous story of the artist engaged to paint the picture of a dying church. Everyone thought he would paint a broken-down tin hut with smashed windows, peeling posters and overgrown grounds. Instead, he painted a fine Victorian Gothic church with beautiful stained glass, elegantly carved pews, an enormous organ and a glorious marble floor. Everyone was bewildered until an old man who had spent much time looking at the painting noticed that down in an inconspicuous corner the artist had painted a small wooden box covered with dust and cobwebs: on it was the label 'For Mission'. Our young friend simply cannot get across to the people of his church that unless the church reaches out, it passes out, and it fills him with divine frustration! But for all the moans and groans that some of them have about Parson Snuffle's preaching, they are quite content to leave it there. For them, a preaching church means that they have a parson who delivers sermons in church on Sunday. Jimmy is trying to tell them that they are wrong—utterly wrong. Until more people in Saint Guthlac's get the message of a preaching church, they will be unable to harness the enormous spiritual energy of Jimmy and those like him—in fact, they may drive him away.

Mind you, Jimmy has got his blinkers as well, like all of us! When Jimmy talks about mission, he means pure spiritual evangelism—telling people the Good News so that they will meet Jesus and put their trust in him, just as he did. For him, mission is verbal preaching of the Gospel pure and simple. But there is much more to it than that, for the Gospel we preach tells of wholeness. You will recall what Jesus read from the prophet Isaiah in the synagogue at Nazareth:

> 'The spirit of the Lord is upon me,
> because he has chosen me to bring good news to
> the poor.
> He has sent me to proclaim liberty to the captives

and recovery of sight to the blind;
to set free the oppressed
and announce that the time has come
when the Lord will save his people.'
Jesus rolled up the scroll, gave it back to the attendant,
and sat down. All the people in the synagogue had their
eyes fixed on him, as he said to them, 'This passage of
scripture has come true today, as you heard it being
read.'

(Luke 4:18–21 and Isaiah 61:1–2)

Whatever the meaning of this text (and Isaiah must have
had the poor exiles in Babylon in his mind and heart), the
gospel of Jesus is not just a message for the soul. Any objec-
tive reading of the New Testament ought to dispel that prejudice. Douglas Webster wrote:

> It is only the fulfilment of its role as a servant that en-
> titles the Church to present Christ to the world it
> serves... The Church and the Christian alike are com-
> mitted to service as the expression of the love and com-
> passion of God in the Name of Jesus Christ. Unless the
> Church is at home in the sphere of service, it is unlikely
> to be relevant when it turns to evangelism.[1]

Jimmy needs to realise that not everyone is converted in his
way, vital as his emphasis on verbal evangelism undoubtedly is. The missionary Church must serve 'and ask for no
reward except that of knowing that we do God's will', for
that is as much the work of mission as is the verbal proclamation of the Gospel. When Jimmy says that the Church
is a preaching people, his definition of preaching should be
wider.

PREACHING WHOLENESS

It will be no surprise to any preacher that the majority of
people who inhabit our churches have an enormous mental

blockage about the whole issue of mission at home, no matter how well or how often attempts are made to get the message across! Let leaders try to tell a church about a decision to initiate a special period of mission, and they will discover that, after several months of struggling to get the message across, there will still be folk who don't understand the first thing about it.

But one mistake Jimmy does not make is to assume that, once you get as far as talking about mission at home, you must mean a few days with a guest preacher when people can stick up posters and dole out handbills to advertise the arrival of this conversion man: as everyone knows, very few new people will come, and most of the time will be spent singing hymns that tell non-believers they believe! Jimmy knows that today most people are converted in small groups, and he knows that commitment to Christ is a costly business; and, we might remind him, most people are converted quite slowly. We have inherited a tradition that understands very little of what it means to be a preaching people.

Since we have noticed earlier that preaching within the context of Christian worship is not where evangelism normally happens, what is the relation between sermons and mission? There are two aspects of this relationship. The first is that we hear the word proclaimed within the Christian family and as we hear the call *'Listen to the word of the Lord!'* so we should be enlisted for action. There is a phrase from the pen of Thomas Cranmer (1489–1556) in the *Book of Common Prayer*, which prays that we may 'hear and receive thy holy word, truly serving thee...' He got it right. We hear God's word; we receive it; and then we turn it into action: what we hear, we act upon, and then we act it out and pass it on.

The second aspect of the relationship between preaching and mission is that the preacher and his people are not separate entities but are part of one body. And that one body is not only spread around the world geographically, but it is also extended over 20 centuries of history. Preacher and congregation together are part of that continuing line of people who have proclaimed and must continue to proclaim the word of the Lord inside and outside the family of the Church. Donald Coggan comments:

> The preacher is not a lone figure, preaching what appeals to him most and leaving the rest unsaid. He is, rather, the last in the apostolic line of those through whose preaching God's salvation in Christ continues. Through him the gospel reverberates.[2]

The sermon has a mysteriously necessary place in the worship of the Church, for it is in proclaiming the word, as much as in celebrating the sacraments or praising or praying, that the people of God become a part of the proclaiming people of the Word. Indeed the Church is a caring body, a sacramental body, a praying body, a serving body, but it is also a proclaiming body. The sermon not only aims to equip the people for their work but it mysteriously begins that work of announcing the Kingdom. Thus the sermon should not be viewed simply in terms of educating or training or advising or even inspiring, unless it is also the worship-centred beginning of all Christian proclamation. What begins here goes on out into the entire world and, we trust, returns eventually like the tide of eternity.

It is, then, the task of the Church as a whole to preach wholeness and to expect the preaching ministry within worship to equip, to educate, and to stimulate God's people for this work. Douglas Webster comments (using the term 'evangelism' in its broadest sense):

> It is quite clear from the New Testament that the very existence of the Church was of evangelistic significance. It was from the outset a community with a difference... Evangelism is always meant to be a joint activity of the whole Church, a shared responsibility...

> In every parish the community spirit should be fostered
> if the parish is to be in action evangelistically.[3]

How many clergy have you and I heard bemoaning the plight of their neighbourhoods? 'If only the people of the area would come to the church. We've tried everything: special services, coffee mornings, expensive advertising, the lot, and still they won't come!' How can these professionals have missed so obvious a fact that until the church, the local church (preferably in concert with all the other local churches) gets out of its comfortable pews and into the homes and shops and work places and dole-queues of the community, it cannot expect anyone to come in? The Church of Jesus Christ is not a self-service filling station: people in our very secular society are not attracted to Christ by religious gimmicks (like the free glasses you get with every tankful of fuel), nor by discipleship at discount price! People come to Christ when the people of the Church get out there and preach with their hearts and their hands as well as with their mouths. The preacher of sermons has the awesome task of communicating this stubborn truth to his people.

There are various aspects to being a preaching people, but none is more important than a commitment to your own locality. It was rural ministry that taught me this lesson—something one learns with more difficulty in the city, though it is equally important there. Whatever your locality, if your church is to preach in it, it must be 100% committed to it and to sharing the burden of its problems. Maybe someone ought to start a playgroup in your church premises for single parents and their children, or open a refuge for people who are on the streets, or start a drop-in centre as an alternative for those who spend their days swallowing 'happiness pills'. Some proper research and a 'mission audit' will help you to define the areas of need. And your church should also want to be committed to the other Christian fellowships in the area: they may not want your friendship; they may not share your convictions, and they may even feel threatened by you (it happens quite often)—but still your preaching church must keep its hand held out to them in love. This is where the local preachers' support group makes a valuable contribution. Most of our urban churches have a considerable proportion of members who come from outside the locality for one reason or another—that is a fact of life today—but that should not deter us from this kind of local commitment. A church founded principally upon the 'gathered community' principle is a church that develops a 'come and get it if you want it' mentality; whereas one that focuses its attention on its locality develops an outgoing apostolic mentality which makes for healthy mission.

In the New Testament we discover all sorts of ways in which the Church preached. Of course, the leading figures are often the apostles, but we should expect that from the nature of the apostolic writings. There is Christian preaching in the synagogues, at least while they remained open to Christians (Luke 4 and Acts 13); preaching by teaching the faith (Acts 19); preaching in homes and families (Acts 10); preaching spontaneously when the right moment came along (Acts 2–5); preaching to individuals (Acts 8 and 9); preaching to non-Jews—quite an issue between Peter and Paul—(Acts 14 and 17); prophetic preaching ('When the prophets are silent and the Word of God is in short supply, the Church withers and dies': Michael Harper) (I Corinthians 12 and 14); preaching by letter (21 of them); and other literature (John 20). The scope of preaching in the first century of Christ was enormous. And the scope for a preaching church today is no less, if only we would face up to the task.

A DEDICATION TO DEDICATION

This book has not been written for great preachers but for the folk like me who find it a most difficult but rewarding task. It has been well said: 'It is not the possession of extraordinary gifts that makes extraordinary usefulness, but the dedication of what we have to the service of God.'[4]

The fulfilment of the preacher's task is when the people in whose company he preaches hear God's word through his ministry and begins to share in the task of preaching: when they themselves begin to call to the world, *Listen to the word of the Lord!*

NOTES

[1] Douglas Webster, *What is Evangelism?* (Highway: London, 1959), p 146.
[2] Donald Coggan, *On Preaching* (SPCK: London, 1978), p 44.
[3] Douglas Webster, *op cit*, pp 130ff.
[4] F W Robertson, *Sermons* (1906).

ADDITIONAL BIBLIOGRAPHY

The number of published sermon collections is considerable and many of them are helpful to dip into. Collections of sermons from a wide variety of preachers, such as P A Welsby's, *Sermons and Society* (Penguin: Harmondsworth, 1970) can be fascinating.

E P Clowney, *Preaching and Biblical Theology* (Tyndale: London, 1961).

F Colquhoun, *Christ's Ambassadors* (Hodder and Stoughton: London, 1965).

B Green, *The Practice of Evangelism* (Hodder and Stoughton: London, 1951).

D T Niles, *The Preacher's Task* (Lutterworth: London, 1958).

J S Stewart, *Heralds of God* (later published as *Teach Yourself Preaching*) (Hodder and Stoughton: London, 1946).

Rolling in the Aisles

Edited by Murray Watts

Tired of the same old sermon illustrations and after-dinner jokes at Christian gatherings? This book is a must for anyone looking for the telling anecdote or the pithy summary to a preaching point.

Illuminating, poignant, and provocative, the short tales in *Rolling in the Aisles* makes our sides ache with laughter. But the humour doesn't stop there; it probes more deeply so that we see the truth about ourselves.

Murray Watts is a playwright and one of the founding directors of the Riding Lights Theatre Company, award winners at the Edinburgh Fringe Festival and famous for a unique blend of comic and serious material. He is the author of several books and many plays, editor of *Laughter in Heaven*, and major contributor to *Playing with Fire*.

Front cover art by Norman Stone.

Foreword by Sir Harry Secombe.

A royalty from every book sold goes to the work of the Children's Society.

Co-published with the Children's Society

160pp   £2.25

Playing with Fire

Edited by Paul Burbridge

Five Stageplays from the
Riding Lights Theatre Company

Wherever the Riding Lights Theatre Company takes its plays, the cast is greeted with high acclaim. Paul Burbridge's selection of plays in this book will prove no exception.

Catwalk – Murray Watts portrays a prisoner of conscience in a Russian psychiatric hospital. Is he or is he not mad because of his faith?

St John's Gospel – Murray Watts' adaptation of the Gospel of John brings fresh insight to the familiar words.

A Winter's Tale – Nigel Forde travels with the Three Magi to show us the hilarious consequences of the gifts brought for the Christ Child – when the Magi meet the local customs officers and the camel has a mind of its own.

Promise – Andrew Goreing uncovers the anguish of a woman suffering from multiple sclerosis who seeks healing.

A Gentleman's Agreement – Murray Watts leads us through the hilarious escapades and misunderstandings of a group of undergraduates on the eve of their graduation.

Five full-length plays that will entertain, challenge and provoke.

256pp   £3.95